Psychic Protection

*-a beginner's guide to safe mediumship
and clearing life's obstacles.*

CRAIG HAMILTON-PARKER

Previously published in 2003 as
Protecting the Soul - Safeguarding Your Spiritual Journey
Sterling Publishing Company, Inc

ISBN-13: 978-1501005640
ISBN-10: 1501005642

Om Gam Ganapataye Namaha

CONTENTS

INTRODUCTION

"Holding as we do that, while knowledge of any kind is a thing to be honoured and prized, one kind of it may, either by reason of its greater exactness or of a higher dignity and greater wonderfulness in its objects, be more honourable and precious than another, on both accounts we should naturally be led to place in the front rank the study of the soul. The knowledge of the soul admittedly contributes greatly to the advance of truth in general, and, above all, to our understanding of Nature, for the soul is in some sense the principle of animal life."
--Aristotle

Words such as spirit, soul, and God are very emotive and may have different meanings to different people. Most dictionaries define the word soul as "the spiritual, rational, and immortal part in man." I suppose you could call the soul our essence. It is the very core of our being-- the part that continues after death and is eternal. It transcends the mind and the moral and emotional part of our nature.

The soul is the seat of innate knowledge and is the source of our conscience. Contained within the vehicle of the spirit, it is the part of us that moves forward on a cosmic journey over many lives. Beginning as a simple spark of God, it grows over many lifetimes from amoeba to human, evolving like a spiritual version of the body's DNA to become the storehouse of our spiritual knowledge and understanding.

This book is designed to show you how to protect this soul essence from negative influences that may inhibit our spiritual progress.

.

1 THE SPIRITUAL MYCELIUM

"If we are interdependent with everything and everyone, even our smallest, least significant thought, word, and action have real consequences throughout the universe. Throw a pebble into a pond. It sends a shiver across the surface of the water. Ripples merge into one another and create new ones. Everything is inextricably interrelated. We come to realize that we are responsible for everything we do, say, or think; responsible in fact for ourselves, everyone and everything else, and the entire universe."

--Sogyal Rinpoche

The studio in the advertising agency was on the second floor and overlooked the city's main street. "Hey, Craig. Do you know this guy," said a co-worker, as he looked down at an odd-looking man in the street below. Unfortunately, I did know him. It was Terry-- someone I had known from my teenage years. Terry had serious psychological difficulties. Some time ago, he had been diagnosed schizophrenic, and he needed a weekly injection to keep him stable. It was plain to see, by the way, he leaned sideways and leered at us that he had missed a few of his treatments again.

Terry was a nice enough character, and I knew he would never harm anyone. He was a person that rarely took risks. I remember, for example, how he gave my friend and me a lift in his car. It took us all day to make the 75-mile journey, moving at less than ten mph along the highway! At the time, he explained, it was a little like the slow-walking meditation used in Vipassana (a Buddhist practice that uses pure self-observation to realize the transient nature of life's activities).

Terry's wife, Dolly, who he met while in a hospital, was also a fascinating subject. She continually wore dark glasses in case of a nuclear flash or other bright lights. Like Terry, she cared intensely about nature. I remember once introducing a friend to them. Unfortunately, My friend did not know about Dolly's concerns and coolly lit a match--something the rest of us would never dare do in the company of Dolly. "Oh my God, the trees! The trees!" Dolly burst out as she fell to the floor and covered her eyes. We made our excuses and left in a hurry. I could sense that this incident was likely to trigger one of Terry and Dolly's surreal disputes, and it was wise not to stay. My perplexed friend never lit a match in their home again.

My colleagues in the champagne and rubber plant world of advertising might not understand my longtime friendship with such suspect individuals. However, "Yes, I know the guy," I responded. "Don't worry about him. He'll get bored soon and will go away."

Two hours later, I decided I had to do something. This was before my mediumistic abilities had fully unfolded, but I was developing a sensitivity to vibrations from other people, and I found it extremely hard to concentrate on work with him down there. Tests in laboratories have revealed that many people can sense when they are being watched. The heartbeats of such subjects will increase slightly even when he or she is consciously unaware they are being stared at. The vibrations coming up from Terry felt like daggers.

My solution, in kind, was to use a mental image to protect myself from the unceasing invasion. I imagined a mirror surrounding me, symbolically blocking my perception of being under spiritual attack. The mirror would both shield me and reflect back the vibrations, allowing me to concentrate. I focused on this image and began to feel more comfortable. Soon I was working as usual, and the next time I looked up from my work, I noticed that Terry had gone.

When lunchtime came, I left the building by the side alley. Terry appeared as if from nowhere and bellowed at me. "How dare you point a mirror at me! How dare you wear a suit and point a mirror at me!" I managed to calm Terry down and explain that just because I was wearing a suit didn't mean to say that I was one of "them." This had worried him (and perhaps rightly). But how did Terry know that I had imagined a mirror? The vibrations he was projecting were real, and the technique I used was an effective counter-measure.

This incident was a practical demonstration of the reality of vibrations and how it is possible to use mental imagery to protect ourselves from negative influences. It was a lesson that has served me well during my years as a Spiritualist medium and psychic counsellor. Besides, it showed me that maybe society judges insanity a little too harshly. I know that Terry and others like him can be deluded, but could it be that sometimes they are aware of real mental energies?

Connecting

" Colour is the keyboard, the eyes are the harmonies, the soul is the piano with many strings. The artist is the hand that plays, touching one key or another, to cause vibrations in the soul."
--**Wassily Kandinsky (artist**)

Have you ever felt vulnerable for no apparent reason? You may normally be reasonably self-assured, but then, right out of the blue, your confidence just evaporates. Often these situations have a psychological cause. You may be overtired, for example, or distracted by your troubles. Perhaps the situation simply reminds you of some past failure. Such unacknowledged anxieties and insecurities can undermine your self-confidence. However, on occasion, hidden spiritual forces may be at work; and sometimes negative energies will temporarily disrupt your inner harmony. Good and bad vibrations come from everybody--not just the mentally disturbed. The feeling of vulnerability comes when you unconsciously recognize unpleasant mental energies coming from the people you meet.

Vibrations of other people also influence the aura, that life force that surrounds us. I sense it visually as an egg-shaped field of multi-coloured light extending about four-feet from the body. It looks a bit like the shimmering heat haze that arises from a hot road on a summer's day. Sometimes, if I am fully "tuned in," I can see that it has a fibrous quality--especially close to the body. I may also notice subtle changes in intensity, with some areas having balls of light or a darkened colouring. From my view of the aura, I can know a person's state of mind intuitively.

The thoughts of others influence your aura. For example, a happy mood can be very contagious. When we are in love, we tend to reinforce each other's energy. When we are with the people we love, our aura's energy increases and expands, giving us a feeling of greater vitality and well-being. On the other hand, those who extend negative energy can make us feel on edge or depressed. We may get a sense of this in the first meetings. Such people may be smiling and appear quite pleasant, for example, but underneath there is a feeling that they cannot be trusted. Shaking a person's hand may increase this awareness. Keep alert at such meetings, and you may find that these "gut" feelings are usually right.

Most of us have become aware of these subliminal vibrations at some point in our lives. I recall occasions when my wife and I visited friends unexpectedly and inadvertently interrupted a quarrel. Of course, they were all smiles when they greeted us and acted as if nothing was amiss. But there was definitely "something in the air." The house felt charged with negativity. Of course, facial expressions, slight changes in tone of voice, and certain body language may offer subtle clues to what is going on, but haven't you also felt pressure surrounding you as you encounter such situations. If you are as psychically sensitive as my wife and I, you will find it almost impossible to remain in these conditions for very long. The aura starts to react to the vibrations. In my case, I experience a tingly sensation, what I can only describe as a "prickliness," all around my body. When this happens, I know I am reacting to more than just sensory clues, but the room's negative energies and emanating from my friends' auras.

You may know people who have potent auras and can project their energy. My father was a classic example. If he was in a bad mood, you felt you could "cut the air with a knife." I remember as a child coming into a room while he was in one of his "simmering" moods. I didn't know it, but he had just finished reading a worrisome letter. Although he was sitting alone in a chair facing away from me, I could tell something was wrong. It was quickly confirmed when he turned around. The thunderous look on his face clearly showed how upset he was. I'm sure that, with a bit of focus training, my father's energy could have caused objects to move or spoons to bend.

Perhaps the above examples of expanded senses are familiar to you. Although you may not claim to be a psychic, you very likely have experienced situations where you have been subliminally affected by people's moods. I believe that we are continually exchanging energy one with another, and these shared energies influence our well-being.

Telepathy

"Another dream-determinant that deserves mention is telepathy. The authenticity of this phenomenon can no longer be disputed today. It is, of course, very simple to deny its existence without examining the evidence, but that is an unscientific procedure which is unworthy of notice."
--Carl Jung (psychologist)

The vibrations we sense from a person are a form of mind-to-mind communication that we call telepathy. Most people think that when telepathy takes place, you "hear" the person's words. We've all watched movies where telepathic messages resonate in a reverberating voice in the background. But most telepathy is not verbal. It comes through shared feelings, emotions, hunches, and images. Because telepathy is a form of communication that pre-dates language, it is challenging to communicate words and numbers telepathically. It is also believed that telepathy emanates from the non-verbal, right hemisphere of the brain--the side that "understands" the world in a holistic, non-rational way.

Many tribal societies today still use telepathy as a part of their daily life. Australia's aborigines mysteriously communicate with each other over great distances and believe that there is a mind link between man and animal. Many hunting tribes in Africa and South America "call" animals to the hunt using mental powers. Tuna fishermen, for example, still entice the fish into their nets by mental command, and to this day, the chief shaman of the Gilbert Islands has the hereditary title of "porpoise caller." His duty, which he enacts at auspicious festival times, is to call the dolphins by telepathy.

Pet owners may believe that they have a telepathic bond with their animals. Our cats Yin and Yang, for example, jump up onto the kitchen windowsill several minutes before my wife Jane or I arrive home. Our dog William used to bark just before our healer friend would phone us, and he would wag his tail at the very thought of the word "walk." Pets indeed appear sometimes to know what we are thinking by responding to those thoughts. And, of course, it is well known that pets lost on a family trip will sometimes miraculously find their way home--even though it means travelling hundreds or even thousands of unfamiliar miles.

It has been argued that pets are very perceptive and may be picking up some unconscious clues from their owners. One suggestion, for example, is that humans may release certain odours in conjunction with intentions, such as deciding to take a walk. Dogs can smell these subtle odours and so respond to them. This may also account for why pets also appear to know if we are ill. There are many recorded cases where dogs, cats, and even rabbits had seemed to know when an owner was about to have an epileptic seizure. These animals may be supersensitive to slight muscle tremors, subtle behaviour changes, or emitted odours that even the victim is not aware of minutes before the seizure takes hold. Anecdotal evidence also suggests that some pets had warned diabetics when their blood sugar was low. Many people believe that dogs can smell cancerous tumours and spots long before such a diagnosis is made.

Rupert Sheldrake, who studied many cases of telepathy between pets and their owners, has made a robust case for animal telepathy. He cites, in particular, the case of a terrier dog named Tiki whose owner knows just when to put on a pot of tea because the dog rushes to stand in welcome on the windowsill whenever his wife is on her way home. The dog responds in the same way, without a clue, even if the schedule is radically changed. Some dogs were found to respond similarly as soon as the owner makes the mental decision to come home! Sheldrake's case studies, surveys, and interviews refute questions about whether dogs can smell or hear their owners approaching. He argues that there is no scientific explanation for the behaviours and, in the absence of some other reason, they must be forms of telepathy. "Some animals do seem to have powers of perception that go beyond the known senses," writes Sheldrake. "But at the same time, many people feel they have to deny these abilities or trivialize them. Pets are the animals we know best, but their most surprising and intriguing behaviour is treated as of no real interest."

Yes, we see telepathy at work in our pets, but similar influences happen between people. It may or may not surprise you, but most people are, to some degree, telepathic. They, however, either pay little attention or don't realize that they are displaying anything in the least remarkable. Do you finish people's sentences for them? Or say the same thing at the same time? You may be displaying mind-reading skills. Perhaps there are times when you seem to know who is calling before you answer the phone. This experience is pervasive. The feeling comes primarily when the caller is a friend or family member-- not if the call turns out to be a stranger or salesman. This is because telepathy's powers work best between people who like each other or, better still, love each other. Laboratory tests indicate that this is true: meaning that, if it happens to you, it is a good sign that a friendship or a relationship is on the right track.

This telepathic "bonding" may have a survival function--in the matter of falling in love and choosing the right mate. Once established, the information communicated in such a strong bond between individuals increases beyond the "feeling" level to include shared imagery and thoughts. This indeed happens between my wife and me. In addition to getting along most of the time, we are both psychic mediums, so the natural telepathy between us is enhanced. On occasion, sent off to the local grocery to pick up some provisions, I return with things I would not usually buy. I recall once, in particular, returning with some silver polish. "Ahh! I'm so glad you got my message," said Jane. "I was sending you a thought to bring some home." Of course, I had no idea that Jane intended to polish the silver, and I certainly had no intension, yet the irresistible urge to buy the polish had popped into my head.

Similarly, Jane "knew" when I had a minor car accident on the way home one evening. Even though I was not hurt and arrived pretty much on time, she met me at the door in some distress, knowing that something had happened. It's bad enough having two cats sensing your arrival, but a wife too!

Couples form natural telepathic bonds that strengthen as they grow to know each other better. They may become aware of each other's thoughts and feelings and remain "connected" even when away from each other. People who love each other and share everyday needs have a strong desire to communicate, which enhances telepathy. This happens between couples, friends, and family members. A mother may sense a child's distress and her desire to protect him readily links with his desperate "calling out" for her. Telepathy is a natural empathy in families or groups where shared needs bond by love.

Telepathy is from the Greek: "tele" meaning "from a distance" and "pathy" meaning "to feel." A perfectly natural skill, telepathy has long been neglected: until now, in our advanced and cell-phone society, it lies largely dormant within the mind. Yet, just as telepathy is familiar and useful between members of certain tribes, telepathy continues to be at work in our own lives. This ancient skill may show itself actively at work or in the home, between lovers or long-ago childhood pals. Most people, however, are unaware of what is happening. Keep alert to events in your life, and you may find telepathy playing a more significant role than you thought. This primal power has a place in our daily lives. It is an emergency lifeline when a group member is in trouble, and its comforting tendrils bind the energies of people who love each other together. Telepathic bonding is a protective force that should not be ignored.

Protective Thoughts

"Listen, there is a hell of a universe next door; let's Go!"
-- e. e. cummings

Telepathy was very useful in ancient times, warning us of danger and providing a link with family and comrades. Yet, apart from a few brave pioneers such as Alfred Russel Wallace (1823–1913) and Sir William Crookes (1832–1919), the early scientific establishment summarily dismissed telepathic powers as nonsense. In 1889, Max Dessoir coined the term "parapsychology", but it wasn't until the 1930's that a systematic scientific study of telepathy was undertaken at Duke University in Durham, North Carolina. Here, some of the most crucial work was done by biologist J. B. Rhine, who established the first scientific laboratory dedicated to psi research. He used statistics to show that, in card-guessing games, some people consistently scored higher than the odds, what one would expect from chance alone. He believed that something was happening beyond the range of our normal senses, and he called these powers Extra-Sensory Perception (ESP).

Since then, scientific work has been undertaken at the scientific community's fringes to investigate the existence of telepathy and other forms of ESP. Experimental methods for studying telepathy occurring during sleep and the dream state were pioneered in 1964 at the Maimonides Medical Center in New York. In 1969 physicist Helmut Schmidt explored the remote influence of both human and animal consciousness on physical systems using radioactive decay.

Telepathy across distances was put to the test in 1973 when U.S. astronaut Edgar Mitchell experimented with mind-to-mind communication while travelling between the Earth and Moon aboard Apollo 14.

A body of scientific research now exists, with the investigation continuing today in places such as the Koestler Chair of Parapsychology in Scotland and, until recently, the 24-year Stargate project funded by the U.S. Government. A Congressionally Directed Action recently induced a declassification of a small portion of the documents. The early work, initiated by physicists Hal Puthoff and Russell Targ, focused on a few gifted psychics, including the New York artist Ingo Swann and former police commissioner Pat Price. They were asked to be "psychic spies" and to use clairvoyance to "see" enemy defence installations. This "remove viewing" technique provided the researchers with some astonishingly accurate information. Also, Swann suggested they try remote viewing the planet Jupiter before the NASA Pioneer 10 spacecraft's upcoming orbit. To everyone's surprise, he reported seeing a ring around the planet--which contradicted all that was known about Jupiter at the time. Soon afterwards, the photos taken by Pioneer 10 revealed an unexpected ring around the planet.

If you study the body of scientific evidence, there is a great deal of proof that ESP, especially telepathy, is real. To this is added our own subjective experiences, which can sometimes be so startling they provide us irrefutable personal proof. The truth is that our thoughts are not limited to our material brains; they "fly" from us. They can travel anywhere to perhaps influence, for good or ill, the minds of others.

Brainwaves

"Cheerfulness removes the rust from the mind, lubricates our inward machinery, and enables us to do our work with fewer creaks and groans. If people were universally cheerful, probably there wouldn't be half the quarrelling or a tenth part of the wickedness there is. Cheerfulness, too, promotes health and immortality. Cheerful people live longest here on earth, afterwards in our hearts. "
-- **Anonymous**

I'm sure that most of the winged thoughts coming to us are

benign, but there are invariably times when negative ones also arrive. Strong thoughts of hatred, such as drawn upon in black magic, may seriously undermine us. Conversely, it is no wonder that some people find fame exciting; the masses' admiring thoughts must be empowering. But, of course, the quality of energy is essential, too. We may think well of a person like Nelson Mandela, but what dark-thought power does a man like Osama Bin Laden crave? These energies play an important role in what drives us.

In the 1960s, a team of Russian scientists discovered that telepathy appeared to influence brain patterns. In particular, funding was made available to study two remarkable telepaths Karl Nikolaiev and Yuri Kamensky. During ESP tests, their brains were monitored, and the team observed the nature of the alpha brain waves that occur when a person is in a relaxed state. Although the two subjects were 400 miles from each other, the studies showed that the normally steady and continuous alpha rhythms of Nickolaiev were dramatically interrupted whenever Kaminsky projected his thoughts to him. Precisely the same results were produced when their roles were reversed.

The experiments revealed that telepathy could disrupt alpha wave patterns. Alpha waves increase when a person is relaxed and may increase dramatically in those who know how to meditate. Alpha is observed in wakefulness when one is both comfortable and effortlessly alert.

A lot of alpha brain wave activity then means lessened anxiety and more likely more developed and more robust immune systems.

I am not surprised at the association of alpha waves with spiritual states of consciousness and human thought transmission. Before I get down to my work as a medium, I need to spend a half-hour in meditation. This quiet time puts me into the right state of mind to accept communications from the spirit people. In meditation, I focus on opening and expanding my aura. I come out of my period of meditation, feeling relaxed and in a cheerful mood. My brainwaves have shifted from the beta rhythms of normal wakefulness to the high-alpha state that follows meditation. Now I can deal with all sorts of negative energy without being affected by it. My client sitters may be filled with grief, anger, pain, despair, and depression, yet these vibrations do not trouble me. It seems to me that we mediums are protected during such contact efforts. If "darkness cannot penetrate light" perhaps it is the high level of the alpha waves we generate that act as our protective spiritual armour. The light of our positive thoughts shines around us, protecting us from any "dark" vibrations. Alpha brain waves are a sign that this energy is in place.

Psychic people are usually cheerful and often gregarious. (Psychic researcher Betty Humphrey of Duke University discovered that extrovert personalities displayed better ESP abilities than introverts.) Most psychics and mediums have a good sense of humour and, despite the troubles in their lives, are generally optimistic about the future. (In 1977, researcher John Palmer examined every published experiment on neuroticism and ESP. He demonstrated that highly neurotic people were poor ESP subjects, and optimists scored better results.) Many psychics are creative and enjoy meditation. All of these qualities are associated with the production of alpha brain waves. Alpha waves are an essential factor in ESP, but they may also explain why we feel protected from negative vibrations when working spiritually. Psychics naturally generate alpha brain waves, which stimulates ESP and acts as spontaneous spiritual protection.

Alpha brainwaves are of use in everyday life as well. A cheerful mood, coupled with inner peace, can protect an individual from commonplace negative vibrations. It seems reasonable then to attempt to increase one's production of alpha waves. One way to do this is through biofeedback techniques. A subject's brainwaves are electronically monitored, and a light switches on whenever alpha waves are being produced. Eventually, the subject learns to recognize the alpha state and can make the light stay on. By becoming aware of when they are in an alpha state, a person can increase the ability to relax and remain cheerful. Biofeedback, besides, has had some success in controlling epilepsy and seizures.

It may be tempting to take a biofeedback training course or invest in special equipment to monitor your alpha waves, but this is not necessary. Some people may find this a quick fix to establishing good mental habits, but I believe meditation is a far better option. Meditation naturally increases alpha waves and can be used at any time and without equipment. In the next chapter, I will provide some simple techniques for entering a meditative state and, in particular, show you how to use the aura to increase your spiritual light.

Working with Telepathy

"Telepathy is not your hearing the words I am thinking in my head; telepathy is when you 'see' what I mean.... the world is not only stranger than you suppose, it is stranger than you can suppose..."
-- **Terence McKenna**

To open my psychic and mediumistic powers, I need to spend time in meditation. This allows me to open my auric field and enter a relaxed and peaceful state of mind. Although my mind remains active, I find that I am no longer bound to my thoughts. In meditation, we discover how to step back from thoughts and become the watcher of our inner processes. I "see" my thoughts appearing in my mind's eye. I observe them, note them but immediately let go of them. Even the most pressing worries and concerns are pointed out with an even-minded acceptance. I remind myself that I can deal with all of these problems later for now is my personal spiritual time.

During meditation, I am in touch with my soul and experience things that are hard to put into words. It is certainly not wasted time, for not only is it more refreshing than sleep, but it also leaves me in a state of heightened awareness. Once in this extraordinary state of consciousness, I connect to my spiritual gifts and the spiritual energies around me. I also feel myself come into contact with the spirit people. On emerging from meditation, I find that I am still connected to the next world. I sense the spirit people's thoughts and feelings and feel my spirit guides and helpers' closeness. These spirit people act as my protection when I do my mediumistic work, which is explained in detail later.

I am fortunate to be one of the few who are aware of our connection to the next world and prove this through my mediumship. I have come to understand that we are all connected spiritually, not only the living with the spirit people, but with each other in this life as well. Unfortunately, most people are completely unaware of this truth and ignorant of the spirit's glorious world around us.

When my gifts are open and active, I become sensitive to the vibrations of other people. At the same time, I am also a bit vulnerable to those with aggressive or upsetting vibrations. I usually can deal with difficult situations and stand firm in an argument if I feel it necessary. When I am tuned in, however, I feel exposed and susceptible to any negativity. This feeling is, at least, unpleasant, and why mediums insist on practising their gifts only in suitable conditions and when surrounded by supportive people. Too, it is unwise to remain in this "open" state indefinitely.

Many novice psychics are eager to open up their spiritual powers and prove them at every opportunity. For this reason, many instructors spend much time teaching how to switch on psychic gifts, but not enough on switching them off again. When mediums remain open, they can become susceptible to people who will drain their energy or unknowingly project negative moods. Staying in this state can be spiritually detrimental. Like a piece of metal being rubbed by a magnet, you too eventually become magnetized by the continual influence of the same negative vibration. Exposure to someone who is depressed can result in you also becoming depressed. I will go into this in more detail later and show you how to reduce these influences.

When I am "open", I become aware of the vibrations of other people. I described earlier how, in meditation, we "stand back" and become an observer rather than a participant in the thinking process. In that state, I am not entirely separated from my thinking, of course, or I would be unable to function. There is, however, a certain amount of disassociation involved. I believe that mediumistic people can carry this "observer" state of mind from meditation into the normal waking state. Measurements taken of the brainwaves of mediums show that they continue to produce high alpha waves levels even after having finished meditation. It is as if the meditative state is drawn forward into daily consciousness.

It is in this state of heightened awareness that telepathy generally takes place. In mediumship, telepathy with the spirit, people sometimes provide information that only they may know. Details are then checked though other sources; that is, to be sure the "new" information is not from the recipient's mind. Telepathy can also take place from person to person. All I have to do is open my mind and observe the thoughts in a similar way to what I described in meditation. Among my thoughts, I will see some that are not my own but are coming to me from an external source. It is a bit like the "light bulb" symbolizing an idea: you may struggle, proverbially in the dark, for ages for the solution to a problem. Suddenly, a creative answer pops into your head out of nowhere and in extraordinary detail. Mediumship and other psychic gifts work in the same way. Ideas appear out of the blue that is very relevant to the person you may be giving a consultation.

Much of this information comes to the medium because the medium and the sitter's auras have blended. This enables a transfer of energy, feelings, and thoughts between them. It could be compared to the way computer networks exchange information. As in an office situation, your computer may be wired to other computers to share files and exchange information, so we can connect to and pass on spiritual info using the auric field. With this telepathic link, we can access one another's memories, thoughts, and feelings. And, just as some computer users may not allow us access, so too a firewall activates when we try to connect to people who are armoured against the possibility of psychic communication.

The Spiritual Mycelium

"No man is an island--he is a holon. A Janus-faced entity who, looking inward, sees himself as a self-contained unique whole, looking outward as a dependent part. His self-assertive tendency is the dynamic manifestation of his unique wholeness, his autonomy and independence as a holon. Its equally universal antagonist, the integrative tendency, expresses his dependence on the larger whole to which he belongs: his "part-ness."

--Arthur Koestler

Nature is a system that works through interconnecting all its parts into a whole. For example, atoms interconnect to form molecules, which in turn connect to form matter and cells, and so on. The gravity from stars and planets draw them together into groups. Similarly, within the brain, trillions of neural interconnections provide a dwelling place for what we call consciousness.

According to the scientist James Lovelock, life on Earth is dependent upon this system of interconnectedness. He called it his Gaia theory, named after the Greek goddess of Earth. Gaia links together plants, animals, bacteria, rocks, oceans, and atmosphere in a unity that shapes the planet and maintains life on Earth. Everything on Earth interacts and depends on one another. Gaia retains just enough water on the planet, counters varying output from the sun, and keeps temperatures within the range that life can tolerate. The Earth is a single, living system, self-regulating in such a way as to maintain the conditions suitable for life on this planet--from near-surface rocks through to the upper atmosphere. It regulates, in particular, the chemistry of the oceans, the composition of the atmosphere, and the surface temperature. A protective layer of ozone is maintained, while the level of atmospheric oxygen is conscientiously kept below the danger point, at which devastating fires would spontaneously break out.

Perhaps one of the most graceful examples of the interconnectedness of living organisms is found in mushrooms and fungi. Mushrooms are the fruiting body of a larger underground organism. They are like an apple growing on an underground tree, with the mushroom itself as just the tip of a huge complex underground network called the mycelium. The mycelium, though active throughout the year, is only revealed by the seasonal appearance of mushrooms. These underground organisms can be huge, covering square miles and growing up to an inch daily. If you could see this mycelium, it would look somewhat like a dense underground spider web covering the entire forest floor. The mycelia web acts as a filtering agent for trees and vegetation, absorbing and carrying nutrients and moisture from areas beyond the reach of needy roots.

All life has similar symbiotic relationships. Everything connects with everything else at all levels, including the mental and spiritual. I have argued that we are all connected on a mental level by telepathy, but the connections we have may be more extensive than this. Could it be that everything is connected together? Perhaps all life is linked in such a way that telepathy is inevitable because everything is naturally connected. We may think of telepathy as a sort of energy wave that flows between us but could it be that telepathy is not an energy? Perhaps it happens because we look within ourselves to that part that is connected to everything else. Within this spiritual mycelium "here" and "there" are the same, so by looking within ourselves we can "see" other people's thoughts or "see" other places and other universes. When we connect to our psychic powers, we are in effect attuning ourselves to our omnipresent soul. This may account for why telepathy can work over any distance without appearing to lose energy, or why some sub atomic particles are influenced by the observer. If we are, as I believe, omnipresent beings, then there is no limit to our perceptions or our reach of consciousness.

In the chapters that follow, we will examine this spiritual mycelium and learn how our thoughts and feelings influence the world around us in a powerful way. I will tell you how thoughts can be used to help others or cause harm: and we will look at ways of protecting ourselves from the harmful thoughts and negative influences that can come to us through this interconnected web of consciousness. In particular, we will study ways to connect to our spiritual center, improve our own thought vibrations, and protect ourselves from those things that inhibit the eternal progress of the human soul.

2 THOUGHT FORMS AND MIND FIELDS

"In every cry of every man, In every infant's cry of fear,
In every voice, in every ban, The mind-forged manacles I hear."
--William Blake

Since the earliest times, people have used ritual and magic to influence the world. The bison drawings from the prehistoric Altamira cave paintings in Spain, dating from 15,000 BC, may have been used in ritual magic to ensure a successful hunt. The principle is that similar things create similar effects--like produces like, or an effect resembles its cause. For example, in black magic, a human being could be cursed to death by spearing a skull with a metal point bearing the name of the intended victim. This imitation of effects to influence events is called sympathetic magic. Magic also holds that things that have once been in contact with each other continue to act on each other at a distance after the physical contact has been severed. Many magic love spells, for example, require that the magician procure samples of the intended's hair or fingernails to be used in the ritual or potion. The former principle is called the Law of Similarity, while the latter is the Law of Contagion or Contact.

I am writing this particular chapter on November 5, when we in the UK celebrate the foiling of the first terrorist attack. Guy Fawkes was a co-conspirator in the "Gunpowder Plot" of 1605 in England. He and his cohorts decided to blow up the Houses of Parliament in London and succeeded in smuggling several gunpowder barrels into the basement. The plot was thwarted, and to this day, we celebrate the occasion by setting off fireworks and burning effigies of Guy Fawkes. This is, in fact, a form of sympathetic magic. Burning an effigy helps people to vent their hatred for their enemies in public. Still, the magician's "law of similarity" also believes that burning the effigy will bring harm to the person whose image is being burnt. (A few years ago, my sister insisted that we burn an effigy of her ex-partner in place of the "Guy")

The ritual of effigy-burning has been found in many ancient cultures, including that of India, Babylon, Egypt, Greece, and Rome. The Ojibway of the American West would fashion small wooden images of an enemy and burn them while chanting magic spells. Called "the burning of the soul," this ritual was believed to bring about the enemy's death. Then, of course, we have all heard of the voodoo doll, into which pins would be inserted to cause an enemy harm. Voodoo is still primarily practised in Haiti, while in New Orleans, rooted in its large slave population mixed with Catholicism, you will find altars set up to protect against hoodoo magic (like voodoo, a primarily healing-based practice based on sympathetic magic).

Sympathetic Magic

"Holy Trinity, punish him who has done this evil and take him from us by thy great justice, that the sorcerer/sorceress may be anathema and we may be safe. Amen."
Popular Hoodoo Spell to remove a curse (To be spoken while throwing *angelica* in a southern direction)

Sympathetic magic is still with us today in our superstitions and beliefs. How often do we see the American flag or effigies of Uncle Sam being burnt in protests? Burning an effigy is pure sympathetic magic: just as the image suffers, so does the man or nation.

Sympathetic magic is not necessarily evil in its intent. For example, voodoo (or more appropriately "Vodu") is a religion that is characterized by ceremony, music, dance, and sacrifice, through which participants commune with their ancestors in trance and possession. It has a pantheon of spirits called Iwa that protect life areas, including love, family health, and wealth. Similarly, throughout Europe and America, there is a growing interest in Paganism's old

18

religion, which is trying to cast off the negative witchcraft image given by Christianity. The truth is that many ancient magical beliefs may be used for good or ill. For example, returning to the effigy theme, puppet healing is the reverse of effigy burning. Instead of desiring to kill or injure the person whom the puppet represents, the practitioner wishes to help them. Healing given to the puppet is transmitted to the person depicted.

Protective healing spells are cast on the night of a full moon by voodoo sorcerers. In particular, they will make a *Paket Kongo* summon the healing spirits. This is an onion-shaped, bright coloured, a cloth-bound package filled with herbs and the powdered flesh of a sacrificed rooster. It is tied around with string seven times and has large feathers sticking out of its top. Similarly, a Catholic may pray in Church with a rosary, or a colour healer may "charge" water or a photograph with coloured light (Graphichromotherapy). It is the intention of the practitioner that determines whether the results of magic are good or evil.

Voodoo and hoodoo have some exciting methods to protect the soul from harm. For example, if a person believes that they are under a psychic attack, they can employ several remedies to negate the damage. They may feel that something "out there" is after them or that someone has bad intentions towards them. Similarly, they may think that this energy has become an "entity", causing bad luck or illness. Wiccans generally believe that once you are aware of the curse or negative energy sent towards you, it no longer has power. In contrast, voodoo and hoodoo followers believe that a curse, spell, or "crossing" can only be lifted using specific rituals and techniques.

Naturally, psychology plays an integral part in making a spell work. Just as we can talk ourselves into being ill, we can frighten ourselves into believing that bad luck and illness will befall us. If we think we are unlucky, we may inevitably attract lousy luck into our lives, and curses may only succeed because the victim believes in their power. Most people find out that they are jinxed through word of mouth or when a "friend" tells them that a spell has been put upon them. Let's face it, people love to gossip, and soon the belief in the jinx is reinforced by the community at large. Inevitably, as soon as something untoward happens to the victim, the jinx is to blame. They may lose their keys or a credit card, and immediately they remember what the friend told them. And so the cycle of fear begins.

Worse still, a hideous token, gris-gris, amulet, or charm may be posted to them or hung on their door to warn them that magic has been cast. A hoodoo sorcerer may nail a gruesome chicken bone amulet on your front door and cover your steps in blood-red powder. In some countries, it is traditional to spit or blow powder in the victims face while speaking curse words. This shocking technique reinforces the curse's power, taking the victim, as it does, off guard and naturally causes severe upset.

Curses and Jinxes

"Protection comes to me this day. This crossed condition goes away. Returning negativity To the one who has crossed me."
--Hoodoo Candle Spell

There are as many ways to remove a curse or spell as there are ways to cast them. These vary according to the cultural tradition of hoodoo. The belief is that curses should be "sent back" to the perpetrator. A popular way of doing this is to scatter *Angelica* in the direction of the curse or the South if the sorcerer is known. Similarly, Five Finger Grass (*Cinquefoil*) can be stuffed into a drained egg sealed with wax. It is believed in New Orleans that a home with this magical egg in it will be free of jinxes and curses.

Followers of hoodoo also like to take special herbal baths made with Dragon's Blood, Five Finger Grass, Ginger, or Pine and Hyssop to protect them from sorcery. Herbs and special powders are also used by the secret "red sects" from Haiti to induce illness and fear in their victims. One pinch of these secret recipes is said to bring bad luck or illness. Similarly, this tradition holds that herbal baths may be used to combat an evil hex and bring luck in love and money. Bath-time food offerings are made to Ezili Freda's spirits (love) or Ibo Lele (money) and may include everything from popcorn to the blood of sacrificed animals. (I would try this technique myself, but I am concerned that my wife would be a little alarmed to see chicken heads among the talc and soaps.)

Haitian voodoo has an armoury of amulets, totems, and tools to protect the soul. Malicious spirits are soothed using an *ason* rattle made from a gourd and containing snake vertebrae. Music and dances are used to counter spells, and many of these ceremonies involve Catholic saints in the rituals. Most Haitian altars, in particular, include a mixture of both voodoo and Catholic imagery, with icons of saints placed alongside tribal gods. Altars also have magical drawings of "verve" designs made during ceremonies to draw the protective spirits from their heavenly homeland to the mortal world. They look very similar to western protective talismans. But perhaps some of the oddest tools of voodoo priests are dolls heads that they squash into bottles to ward off evil spirits and sequined bottles decorated with the Gede spirits' skull motifs (the guardians of the dead and masters of the libido). Franz Barra created one strange protective totem, featured a Barbie doll squeezed into a miniature, red-sequined coffin.

The Evil Eye

Of course, voodoo and hoodoo are not alone in giving strange, surreal remedies to protect the soul from curses and spells. Many believe that a jealous stare or envious glance can harm the soul. The eyes are considered "the gateway to the soul" and, in many cultures, the "evil eye" is believed to harm the soul. It is one of the oldest and most culturally prevalent magical beliefs in the world. The evil eye is believed to cause miscarriage, illness, business failure, marriage breakdown, bad luck, and a great many misfortunes. Besides, anyone, including those who have no special powers, can give the evil eye. Since it happens involuntarily, no one can be certain who or where the evil came from, making this one of the most feared of all magical powers. People with different coloured eyes or eyes set close together or deep in their head were often suspected of having the Evil Eye and were often persecuted as witches from the sixteenth to the eighteenth century. In the 1930s, a man from New York earned his living by renting his evil eye to prize-fight managers. He would sit ringside and stare at opposing fighter.

There are hundreds of ways to avert the Evil Eye. One of the most immediate techniques, and not recommended for dinner parties, is to spit three times in the eye of the onlooker. Another is to step aside if someone is staring at you, so letting the negativity pass you by. The Italians wear special amulets of hands, making sexually symbolic gestures for protection from the evil eye: called the mano fico ('fig hand) or the mano corunto (horned hand). In most cultures, the cure involves a complex series of rituals, which vary around the world. Water, oil, and melted wax often play a part, or the practice may centre on an eye-shaped and liquid-filled natural object such as an egg. Animals that were supposedly affected by the Evil Eye were burned, after which the person who had made the curse would suffer the same agony. Similarly, a clay manikin, or witch puppet, made in the suspect person's likeness with the Evil Eye would be stuck with pins to lift the spell.

Naturally, I have always believed these things to be hocus-pocus; that is until my Israeli friend brought us a present from his homeland. He knew we had trouble with a neighbour, so he gave us an ornate hand in the "stop" gesture with an eye in the palm. "This will avert the evil eye of the bad woman," he said. "It's good. Hang it up in front of your house, and you will have no more trouble."

Within three months, the bad neighbour had moved.

Profits of the Prophets

"Praying is like a rocking chair--it'll give you something to do, but it won't get you anywhere."
-- **GYPSY ROSE LEE** (Rose Louise Hovick, American stripper)

Many people claim that sympathetic magic is "mumbo jumbo", and that results can be explained away. This is undoubtedly true in some instances, but there are also times when such magic appears to have worked. Yes, belief alone may be enough to cure some people or fulfil a spell's curse. But there are cases on record that contradict that scenario--where people appear to falter even though they are unaware a curse has been placed on them. Nonetheless, common sense is the primary ingredient in spiritual ventures, particularly concerning magic and the healing arts. Some people, for example, believe that snake bite calls for treatment by "magic snake stone," which is, in reality, no more than benzoin or a gallstone, having no effect on the venomous bite. If a snake-bitten person were to rely on such magic in this instance, consequences could be fatal.

Sadly, charlatans still exist today to take advantage of those who are gullible and superstitious. Often this is the case with those who are upset about the break-up of a relationship: they will do, or pay, anything to get their partner back! A common scam is promising to change your luck by lifting a curse or a jinx or removing "negativity from your aura." Through my columns and website, I have received many letters from people frightened by threats of a curse that they are told can only be removed if they pay money. These "psychics" often target people who are already fearful, having encountered "bad luck" in their lives. The fraud psychic have good observational skills and can provide the sitter with enough apparently valid information to convince them that what they say is true. They are alert to facial reactions and bodily gestures and incorporate feedback information likely mentioned earlier in the sitting or consultation or hinted at in response. Once the sitter is hooked with this "cold reading," the charlatan may offer to change the person's luck for a price. I know of someone who was quoted $3,000 to have bad luck lifted from their lives. For this fee, the "psychic" would burn a magic candle to clear the misfortune. However, she warned that it might be necessary to burn additional candles as the case was terrible. Of course, this would necessitate added costs for the magic candles and her services.

A real curse is a set of words or a ritual that has been imbued with the negative energy of a thought-form. A curse cannot harm us unless we allow it to give the negative energy an entry point. Indeed, paying money to someone else will not remove negative energy or have rituals performed on your behalf. The key to protection from real curses come from your refusal to give in to superstition and unfounded fear. Just as money can't buy you, love, giving money to such people cannot change your luck or make you well again.

People often incur such problems when they do not generally take personal responsibility for their lives. They tend to go to a fortune-teller because they want someone else to make the hard choices for them. It is much easier to blame things outside of ourselves for our troubles. We accuse others instead of owning up to our faults. We blame circumstances and people for problems that are of our own making. And, of course, many of us blame our bad luck on fate. How much better it is to take charge of our own lives! Personal responsibility gives a person self-confidence and a realistic view of circumstances. The right psychic role is to provide insight and inspire, not to make decisions for you. A psychic can encourage you and even empower you to take charge of your destiny. To do something about it! So, take my advice: If you are ever asked for money to remove a curse or a spell, to regain health, to bring back a lover, or to change your luck, leave immediately and don't look back!

Magical Entrapment

One particularly nasty incidence of being ripped-off happened to a Sunni Moslem friend from Lebanon who used to sit in my mediumistic development circle. The problem with this incident was that the con-woman had real magical powers to entrap people. Tareque is an intelligent, honest man who has a senior position within the medical profession. He had initially come to me for a private consultation, and the sitting had gone very well. I immediately picked up that he worked with facial reconstructive surgery and had come from someplace where many bombs were exploding. In relaying the results of the sitting later, Tareque said, "Craig told me that my family was on vacation in Tyre but had not had time to tell me about it. He also told me that my younger brother would be selling telephones and visiting our uncle in the Gulf to talk about it. Craig correctly said he was a very devout Muslim, wore white, preferred sitting on the floor and, unlike most Arabs, has bright blue eyes. My other brother was now in America, and I had a sister in Canada. Craig told me all my family's movements, who I had not heard from for six months. Two days after the sitting, I had a call from my sister in Canada who wanted to tell me all the latest news. For fun, I decided to speak first: 'How was mother's holiday in Tyre? Has our brother gone to the Gulf? Does he enjoy selling telephones?' I told her everything Craig told me. 'How on earth do you know all this!' she exclaimed...but that was my little secret."

Sometime after that consultation, when Tareque joined my development circle, we got to know each other better. He was honest and intelligent. He had come from a scientific background and was not a person prone to fantasy, yet the story he confided was like something out of Faust. At times, as he told this tale, he visibly shook with fear, and his swarthy skin looked ashen.

It started while he was living in his home country of Beirut. He met and regularly visited a woman fortune teller who eventually offered to train him. The woman's particular interest was to call upon elemental spirits and use them to draw money and power to her. Elementals are nature spirits associated with the "elements" of mysticism: earth, air, water, and fire. According to ancient astrology and magic, each person is born with an affinity to a particular element. There are spirit guardians for each of these elements, supernatural beings that watch over people and places associated with their specific element.

It was decided that Tareque should have a fire elemental as his protector. Together, fortune teller and student spent many nights in front of an open fire in the desert working to summon the ancient fire spirits. At first, when he saw something moving in the flames, Tareque thought he was hallucinating. But, he explained to me, he was completely lucid and watched in astonishment as a small six-inch tall man began to crawl around in the embers. The "figure of fire" eventually climbed out of the flames and stood before him, glowing like the embers. Tareque explained that the animated mannequin looked like a Roman soldier. It also filled his heart with such absolute terror that he knew he had summoned something terrible. His teacher's response was to increase the fear further. "Once you have summoned this genie," she said, "he is with you forever. Only I can make his return."

Unfortunately, my friend was at the woman's mercy. She demanded money from him to remove the demon. He paid the small fortune but never contacted the woman again.

Demons and Elementals

"We work in the dark. We do what we can to battle the evil that would otherwise destroy us. But if a man's character is his fate, it's not a choice but a calling. Sometimes the weight of this burden causes us to falter. From the fragile fortress of our mind. Allowing the monster without to turn within. We are left alone staring into the abyss. Into the laughing face of madness."
--AGENT MULDER (from The *X-Files*)

In European and American Wicca, demons and elementals are summoned either through invocation or Demonic mediums. Typically, sorcerers rely on pentagrams to protect them during a lengthy summoning ritual. After the rituals, the sorcerer must engage in a test of wills with the summoned being to determine whether it is under the sorcerer's control. If the sorcerer loses the test of wills, the summoned being may attack the sorcerer.

An elemental requires a sustaining environment. In Tareque's case, this was the element of fire. Elementals can assume many forms, such as small animals or miniature versions of natural phenomena such as whirlwinds, flames, fountain, and so on. However, their power is not autonomous. If we withdraw our attention, the elemental eventually loses its strength and disappears from the material world. Sorcerers claim that elementals do not "die" as such but retain their consciousness and memories of events. Some only remember basic things, such as positive or negative feelings for familiar persons, locations, and events.

The way to protect yourself from these negative thought forms is to limit the mental energy that you extend to them. I believe that there are such things as demonic and elemental spirits, but we are naturally protected from them in general life. When mediumship is developed in the right way, our protection is greatly increased. The aura radiates a protective light that allows only benign and beautiful spirits to penetrate. Summoning demonic spirits is, in my opinion, the playground of fools and schizophrenics. Based on the people I have met, black art followers are usually on a very odd ego trip, and they are sometimes involved in unhealthy sexual activities. Still, their powers cannot harm us if we follow a path of light and sincerity. Although I am able to commune with the spirit world, I have never felt threatened by the demons that supposedly possess some people and places. Protecting yourself from their unholy influence is easy. You simply refuse to feed them with your fear or attention and walk with confidence, knowing that darkness cannot penetrate the light. It is light that penetrates the darkness.

Thought Forms

"Matter is a development of thought, crystallized mental energy"
--EVANS-WENTZ

Much of the phenomena considered so far are founded on superstition and anxieties resulting from not taking personal responsibility for your life. However, studies have revealed that the mind can influence matter and sometimes create forms with its own will. Pioneering in this research was parapsychologist Joseph Banks

Rhine, who gave us the term Extra Sensory Perception. He was one of the first to investigate psychokinesis (mind over matter). In the 1930s, Rhine set up the world's first laboratory in North Carolina to study parapsychology. Some of his most interesting experiments involved a professional gambler who tried to prove that it was possible to influence dice's fall by willpower. Various of these early tests were criticized for lack of scientific safeguards. Still, more stringent experiments have been carried out in more recent years to qualify the results of these pioneering studies.

By its very nature, this type of experimentation is likely to attract criticism, and the jury is still out regarding its authenticity. One of the best-known cases of psychokinesis is the spoon bending of Israeli psychic Uri Geller. His powers have been tested in controlled conditions at Stanford Research Institute in California, and he underwent tests at 17 different laboratories. Some of the most thorough testings were conducted in Britain by two academics from London University, Professor John Taylor of King's College and Professor John Hasted of Birkbeck College. Similar PK effects may occur around ordinary people in the form of objects moving or poltergeist phenomena. Indeed, there is a great deal of evidence that it exists, and I have personally seen things move on their own in my séances.

Psychokinesis, however, may not be limited to bending spoons or making objects move. Many believe that mental energy can create thought forms that continue to exist for a while, even after the psychic has finished working. Thoughtforms could act in the same way that we would expect a spirit entity to manifest. They have a semblance of personality and appear to be semi-conscious. One exciting example happened in Toronto, Canada; the case involved a poltergeist known as Philip. In this instance, a group consisting of eight members of the Society of Psychical Research decided to invent a ghost named Philip and then try to summon it. They worked out Philip's history and background. He would be a contemporary of Cromwell, who had an affair with a gipsy girl who was then burned at the stake when she was accused of witchcraft. Hearing the news of her death, the fantasy person, Philip, killed himself by throwing himself off the battlements.

After many sittings, the group was able to contact Philip using table tilting. The table would make a knocking sound in answer to questions and repeated the story that had been invented for him. The phenomena were so strong that a television crew was able to film the table dancing around the room on its own when it was under the entity's influence.

Some argue that this phenomenon (and all other Spiritualist phenomena) result from unconscious mental forces created by the group's mind. Others say that an independent spirit had moved the table and obliged the sitters by impersonating Philip. I believe that Philip is likely to be an example of a mind-generated "thought form" that can evolve and take on a mind of its own.

There are many examples of this in occult history. The Tibetans, in particular, called thought-forms *tulpas*. Once a tulpa is created, clairvoyant people can see it. The female explorer of Tibet, Alexandra David-Neel, documented this phenomenon at length in 1931. While living with and studying the Tibetans, David-Neel herself used secret meditation techniques to create a jolly fat monk's tulpa.

In time, the tulpa grew in power and became indistinguishable from physical reality. Eventually, David-Neel lost control of it, and the monk would appear against her will. Her fat monk became thinner and was now manifesting with a distinctly sinister aspect. He was as solid as you or I and could now be seen by everyone. David-Neel decided things had gone too far and applied different lamaist techniques to reabsorb the creature into her own mind. Unfortunately, her spiritual companion had now evolved into a troublesome entity, and it was challenging for her to dissolve it. It took six months of ritual and meditation and left her exhausted. Afterwards, she said: "There is nothing strange in the fact that I may have created my own hallucination. The interesting point is that in these cases of materialization, others see the thought-forms that have been created."

Protection from Negative Thought Forms

"The power of the imagination may produce diseases in man, and it may cure them."
--PARACELSUS

The creator of a thought-form can lose control of it and, once created, take on a life of its own and operate independently. If you believe that an independent thought-form is hindering you, there several ways to deal with it:

1. Do not feed it.

Thought forms are sustained by the energy we give them. Although they may appear to have an independent reality, they are in fact, a product of our mental energy. Suppose the thought-form becomes troublesome energy, as in the instance of the *tulpa* described earlier, the key to dissipating it is to withdraw your attention from it. Ghost and poltergeist activity will often disappear if we ignore the troublesome phenomena.

2. Have no fear.

Your fear will increase the power of a thought-form. It also feeds it with precisely the wrong sort of energy and only makes matters worse. It is better to fill the affected environment with positive energy. For example, one of the best ways to clear a haunted house of negative energy is to throw a party. This will fill the place with the happy energy of people enjoying themselves. Naturally, it is better not to mention that you have any problems, so that people's attention is directed at having fun rather than on the negative thought-form.

3. Use positive imagery.

Traditionally, curses and black magic are countered by performing rituals or by making special potions, sacred objects, and amulets. You may feel comfortable calling a priest or other specialist to perform protective rituals. All of these remedies strengthen your faith and give you confidence that something constructive is being done to overcome the energies afflicting you. They help you to build a more positive attitude to combat the negative thought-forms. Your inner attitude is all-important; it is up to you to send positive thought-forms of your own to transform your environment eventually. You could surround yourself with imagery that has a personal appeal to you. For example, I prefer to hang up a picture of Mickey Mouse to lift my spirits and thoughts than some sombre protective symbol of magic and religion. It is the inner attitude that counts when generating positive thought-forms of your own.

4. Be Spiritual

Following a spiritual path will naturally strengthen your aura and protect you from negative influences. This need not necessarily involve religious practice, for no religion has a monopoly on truth. A sincere search for God or a humanitarian attitude will create the right mental energy to protect you from negative vibrations automatically.

5. Have faith in yourself

I have argued that one of the most important things we can do is to take personal responsibility for our spiritual progress. If you accept that most of the troubles you have are of your own making, you empower yourself to solve them eventually. This discipline can create invincible energy.

We will look at some of the above in detail later in the book and other practical techniques such as Feng Shui, meditation, yoga, and mental exercises to increase your natural protective energies.

Extended Consciousness

"We cannot live only for ourselves. A thousand fibers connect us with our fellow men; and along these fibers as sympathetic threads, our actions run as causes, and they
come back as effects."
--HERMAN MELVILLE

Some mystics have taught that thought is a physical thing. They claim that every particle of matter has a particle of mind energy connected to it, and by picturing in mind a particular object, a thought-form is created in the shape of the object perceived. In this way, a material thing can be materialized by focusing on the mental image and gathering together thought forms connected to individual particles of matter. This technique, which I have witnessed, requires a degree of spiritual power that ordinary people do not possess but which some mystics master after many lifetimes of arduous practice. Similarly, the reverse is true, in that matter can be infused with mental energy. An idol, for example, may take on extraordinary powers because of the thoughts projected into it by worshipers: consider a statue or image of the Hindu god Ganesh drinking milk or a Catholic's Madonna crying.

The American psychic Edgar Cayce believed that thought is tangible. He spoke about how thought was a finer form of matter and how thoughts have different densities. This also corresponds to many of the ideas within Spiritualism. The rate of thought vibration dictates spiritual advancement. Fast vibrating thoughts are associated with love and compassion and naturally rise to the paradise planes of the next world. Selfish and hateful thoughts are slowly vibrating. They are sluggish and "heavy" and so sink towards the lower afterlife worlds.

After death, we are drawn to the level of existence that corresponds with our vibration's overall rate. Heaven and Hell are varying levels of vibration that correspond to our own positive or negative thought. Therefore, compensation or retribution is determined by our inner state, which, fortunately, can be changed through the power of our own free will. From a Spiritualist's perspective, the cosmic plan is not to punish humanity but to encourage the soul's continuous evolution through free will. Similarly, in our earthly world, the higher vibrations of love and compassion will protect us from the negative vibrations of hate, jealousy, and so on.

I have spoken already about how thought can extend from us and sometimes even form separate entities. My spiritual mentors, who speak through me in a trance, have also told of this. They have given many discourses to explain that all thought is inter-connected, forming a whole. Every idea we have connects to everything else and thereby influences the whole.

My spirit guides have spoken about what they call the mycelium of consciousness. It works the same way the roots of a group of mushrooms connect over a large area. We may also compare it to the Internet, where many separate computers link together. When I work as a psychic medium, I become aware of this interconnectedness. To access the "network," I only have to look within, to my thoughts, and check for "incoming messages." I may sense thoughts being given to me by the spirit world or notice that my perceptions can extend to remote view distant places. Just as I can connect with the whole world with an Internet-linked computer, so too, I can access the collective web of consciousness when I link my thoughts to the spiritual mycelium. Once connected to the inner web, it is possible to communicate with the spirit world: see remote locations, access the past, and view future possibilities. I believe there is no limit to the information it is possible to access using these clairvoyant skills. Psychic mediums are the pioneers of a great adventure that will eventually become the spiritual domain of everyone. With proper training and motivation, I believe that, in the future, many people will learn how to access these other levels of reality.

Creative people are often aware of this extended consciousness when ideas simply "come to them." Usually, there is a feeling that an idea has come from out of nowhere, landing completely on their lap. Could it be that some ideas--particularly the great ones--are independent thought forms given to us via the spiritual mycelium?

There are undoubtedly many instances of inventions and discoveries made within moments of one another. It's as if a thought form has been created and, on its own accord, it will now seek to become a reality. I believe that essential ideas often are given to us by something outside of ourselves: the collective unconscious, spirit influences, or maybe part of the mind of God. Many great inventions have come independently to several people simultaneously, even though there is no way they could have known about each other's intentions. For example, Alexander Graham Bell invented the telephone and filed patent number 174 465 on February 14, 1876. Only 3 hours later, Elisha Gray, a different inventor working entirely independently, filed another telephone pattern. Within two years, there were 600 lawsuits against the patent, coming from people claiming they had invented it first.

Mind Fields

"When we try to pick out something by itself, we find it hitched to everything else
in the universe."
-- JOHN MUIR

Every thought you have influences the cosmos. Your brain will remember your thoughts, feelings, and sensations, of course, but your thoughts also leave an impression on the cosmic mycelium. Persistent thoughts and desires will generate energies that will influence the course of your life. If you have a sustained willingness to become an artist, for example, the energy created will eventually bring you opportunities to pursue this goal. Your mental powers draw these opportunities to you, and it is then up to you to act upon them or not. As found in prayer, meditation, mantras, and affirmations, carefully focused thought act upon the cosmic mycelium in a sustained way and hastened the process. In my own life, I have found that once a vision of what I hope for is set in my mind, the cosmos acts upon my desire to bring these things to me. In particular, I believe that wishes for spiritual things come more quickly than material desires because the soul has a long-sighted and hidden agenda for our true happiness.

The same also applies when groups of people work together for a common purpose. The collective hopes build mental energy that brings fulfilment of the desire. Again, I believe that collective desire for spiritual blessings come more quickly than material gain. So why are we not living in a utopia? The fact is that most people's hopes and desires are not for spiritual things. Their desires are greedy and bring with them blessings, but also problems. If people's hearts were to change, I believe that we would soon have a Golden Age. Unfortunately, it is not easy to change people's hearts.

I call these collective group energies a "mind field." You no doubt noted the pun on the word "minefield." Indeed, these group energies are often unstable or may be problematic for us. These mind fields work within crowds, businesses, institutions, and countries and in intimate relationships, friendships, and families. Small and large groups of people generate their mind field that will influence their collective destiny.

I have already mentioned how right spiritual motivation can create a potent mind field. A spiritual mind field also creates powerful protective energies that trigger spiritual advancement or the development of psychic, healing, or mediumistic powers. The energy in some of the early Spiritualist circles was so powerful that materializations and aports were commonplace. In particular, these powerful mind fields enabled the pioneer mediums to manifest a substance called ectoplasm that would mould into the recognizable features of spirits communicating from the afterlife.

I have been running my mediumistic development circle for over ten years. Many of my original trainees have now progressed to become professional mediums, psychics, and healers. I have seen many group field changes as my fledgeling mediums leave the nest and new pupils join me. It is fascinating to see how the energy of our very powerful mind field changes and adapts over the years.

Sitting in a dark room and communicating with the spirit world may sound a bit frightening to anyone who has never attended a séance. I remember, for example, how the congregation shook with fear outside their Spiritualist Church at our wedding. I'm sure many of them thought that we would take our oaths over an Ouija board! But once a person experiences the uplifting vibrations of a Spiritualist service or a private séance, they soon understand that these things are far from frightening. The energy is soothing, inspiring, and has a healing quality that brings us close to the divine.

The first part of my weekly séances includes a period of meditation. I play a CD of my voice, with appropriate musical accompaniment, that leads people into a relaxed state and encourages them to open up their spiritual energy centres, called the chakras (explained in detail in chapter 6.) We then sit in silence. As we sit in the candlelit room with our eyes closed, we begin to feel the room's atmosphere change. We think of ourselves enveloped in warm, gentle energy that restores our vitality. We sense our auras joining to form a protective circle of light. We feel the spirit guides and helpers draw close during this time, giving reassuring messages and guidance about our spiritual progress. Working as a medium can be extremely exhausting work, but these sessions allow me and my group time to become quiet and recharge. It also allows us a little time to be alone with God.

Strangers to these proceedings may think that a séance is a

dangerous place, one where you are exposed to weird entities and spirits. However, if the sessions are held with the right motivation and objectives, the opposite is true. A properly conducted séance is a place of spiritual safety. Not only are you protected from any negative paranormal influences, but you are also protected from the day-to-day negativity of ordinary life. If someone thinks ill of you, their winged thoughts may affect you. However, in a séance setting, you are protected by the circle of light I described earlier and, more importantly, by the thoughts of love that the sitters, and their loved ones in spirit, share.

Even though the members of my sitting circles have changed over the years, energy has been created that persists even though original members have left. Every time we sit to meditate, we awaken the shared energy that has been growing with my groups over the years. It is an energy that is available to us every time we start to work, and it will presumably continue until the group stops meeting for a prolonged period. It is a self-sustaining mind field.

Sometimes we experiment by moving this energy around the room in a clockwise or anti-clockwise direction. We may focus it on one person or use it to generate energy spirals. Moving energy in this way helps us to let the energy flow in our auras. This is good for our health, as it allows the healing power to flow through our auras. Many therapists, such as acupuncturists, believe that illness is caused when the life force's flow is blocked in some way. Allowing prana to flow in this way helps to loosen the energy blocks and promotes better health. It is a fascinating experiment to try, and we have even used the power to move objects-- such as a small strip of paper floating in a bowl of water.

Similar energy has developed around my website community. We have built a password-protected chat-room area where people meet to develop their spiritual powers. Here we hold online workshops and run small mediumistic circles where people can connect and learn to link with the spirit world. Remarkably, we have discovered that now there is energy joining us that appears to take no notice that we are logging in from all around the world. We have tried moving this spiritual energy between ourselves and become aware of one another's vibrations or state of mind. We have used this energy to practice telepathy and mediumship.

Absent healing is possible when we link together in this way. For example, if one of our members feels ill, we concentrate on sending them positive healing thoughts. We may do this by using a guided meditation in which we visualize the person enjoying a beautiful setting and surrounded by healing light. We send our thoughts, and healing energy follows that thought to the recipient. Similarly, we have sent protective energy to those who feel that they have been under a psychic attack or who may feel vulnerable because of their problems. Our collective thoughts of compassion and healing can act as a catalyst for change, enabling them to pick themselves up and carry on. Of course, when you feel the need for protective healing, you may imagine an emerald green, electric blue, or white healing light enveloping you and filling your body with sparkling energy. Negative energy and illness are banished from your body, mind, and soul.

Once, the group tried sending me energy when I had the flu. I became aware of how my energies immediately lifted from their healing rays. It is a remarkable feeling to sense this positively charged mind field of loving energy. Many people on the site have perceived it and felt it as a positive influence. When a group of healers concentrate upon you--even over a great distance--there is a marked feeling as the healing energy restores you. It is a real sensation and not a trick of the imagination or a psychosomatic effect. The energy makes you feel better. The same technique works when we send energy to ill people who are entirely unaware that we are focusing on them. They make surprisingly quick recoveries.

The mind fields between spiritually linked people are very powerful, yet similar energies also exist between individuals, within business organizations, in a church, or even encompassing a nation. In later chapters, we will show how these mind fields can protect and nurture us and how best to deal with energies detrimental to our well-being.

3 NEGATIVE ENERGY FIELDS AND COUNTERS

"Treat the earth well: it was not given to you by your parents; it was loaned to you by your children. We do not inherit the Earth from our Ancestors; we borrow it from our Children."
--Ancient American Indian Proverb

When you first bought your home or made plans to rent your apartment, many factors influenced your decision. You likely sought guidance from your real estate agent and attorney, perhaps a surveyor or appraiser, and considered the cost, size, amenities, and location of the property. The one factor, however, that influenced your choice above all else was that gut feeling that the place "felt right." You had a hunch that this was it! Other properties may have had bigger rooms or more conveniences, but the deciding factor was that it "felt like home." If we trust these gut feelings, we usually make the right decision about where to live.

I believe that archaic peoples used their instincts in this way. Tribal societies such as the Aborigines or the Native Americans lived in harmony with their environment. They could sense where to find water in the desert or know if certain places were Bad Lands. They sensed which areas had dangerous animals, snakes, or insects, and their gut feelings would alert them to environments where it was dangerous to sleep. Our instinct of "feeling at home" may originate from those times. It is our intuition letting us know that the environment is safe.

Could the environment contain vibrations that alert or warn us about areas, whether safe or harmful? If you are sensitive to people's mind-fields, you may also be sensitive to the energies that thoughts imprint on the environment. For example, I used to work late and would take a shortcut home through the graveyard at the dead of night. Even with my understanding of the spirit world, I have to admit that this Victorian graveyard was a spooky place with its broken statues and stones. It had a frightening atmosphere. Some areas retain the mind field generated by people's intense emotions at these locations. Graveyards are full of the vibrations of grief as well as our fears of death. Similarly, they say that no birds sing at the extermination camp of Belsen, where Anne Frank and thousands of other Jews died. Belsen is clouded in vibrations of horror left by the memories and feelings of the Jews, Gypsies, and Poles that perished there.

Many of the ordinary places you visit also have an atmosphere of the people that once lived and died there. A church or temple may feel peaceful and uplifting because of the many years of worship, and an old school building may still buzz with the excitable vibrations of children. Battlefields may reverberate with memories of ancient carnage, and old buildings may always whisper with the voices of people long gone. If you were to be blindfolded and secretly taken to one of these places, you would probably sense a unique atmosphere in the air. You would have a gut feeling of the vibrations that still haunt these scenes.

The truth is that mind fields will continue to influence an environment for many years after the occupants have gone, and these energies may be helpful or harmful to us. Sometimes people may get an evident impression of these mind fields and witness events in the past. My newspaper and Internet columns have drawn many people to write to me telling me they have "seen history." For example, one writer spoke of how she saw someone knifed in her front room. Only later did she find out that her house was the scene of a gruesome murder fifty years earlier.

Similarly, a Scottish firefighter wrote to tell me how, while fighting a fire in Edinburgh, he saw scenes of the building that had stood there a hundred years before. He saw a Victorian workhouse with lines of people waiting to be fed. "I was transported back in time and saw the lines of flotsam and jetsam queuing up, and I heard many different dialects spoken," says Harry from Edinburgh. "I became aware of the struggle that these poor people lived with and sensed their presence all around me. This vision of despair was so powerful that it has stayed with me all of my life."

Vibrations of the Battlefield

"I have sworn upon the altar of God, eternal hostility against every form of tyranny over the mind of man"
--**THOMAS JEFFERSON**

There have been many reports from people who have seen ghostly knights in armour still fighting on history's battlefields. In France, it is said that are knights yet seen falling beneath English arrows at the site of Agincourt; in Scotland, the soldiers still wail on the fields of Bannockburn and Culloden. England has its phantoms of the fallen cavaliers of the English Civil War, Belgium its ghosts on the Somme, and on a still night at Stalingrad, it is said you can hear the ghostly echoes of the sounds of war.

Wherever massive deaths and violent confrontations are mixed, the chance is that these events' vibrations will be present in the area. The violence and fear associated with sudden death still linger, but I consider it unlikely that earthbound souls continue to fight battles in the astral plane. Instead, these phenomena are mind-field recordings that persist as vibrations are perceived by visitors who may have latent psychic potential.

The American Civil War was one of the bloodiest wars ever fought. Since it was waged totally on American soil, it pitted brother against brother, family against family, and nearly split the country in two. Approximately one million men were killed or wounded. It is, therefore, no wonder that some of these battlefields are the most haunted in the world.

An exciting example of sensing mind fields happened when Carole, one of my first psychic UK helpers on my chatroom, decided to meet up with our American helper Jean. "One evening, during the vacation, Jean took four of her friends and me to visit the 'Devil's Den' near her home in Pennsylvania," says Carole. "It was a famous battle site of the American Civil War. Darkness was drawing in when we arrived. We both had a feeling of foreboding about the place. We felt as if we were walking through something simultaneously and then had the eerie feeling that something was right behind us. I spun around and took a photograph.

"The weird feelings got worse as we came to the area called the 'Slaughter Pen,' which is a forested area with a small path running through the trees. At this place, thousands of soldiers had been trapped and killed. The feelings there that night were dreadful. It was such an oppressive atmosphere. If Jean and the others hadn't been there, I'd have run for it. Although it was a desolate and lonely spot, we sometimes could hear people whistling tunes. I took some more photographs.

"The next night, we went to the nearby battlefield at Gettysburg to a place called 'Spanglers Springs.' This place was another part of the battlefield, but it was supposed to be a neutral area where the soldiers from both sides could drink. However, fighting broke out, and hundreds were killed.

"This time, Jean brought along six of her friends to keep us company. Again we started to feel a strange atmosphere. Suddenly we heard these strange calls, like a whooping followed by weird animal calls. Later we described it to an expert who takes part in civil war re-enactments, and he told us that what we heard was called the 'rebel yell.' It was what the rebel soldiers used to do to try and scare the union soldiers. We had all heard it, yet it was clear that there was nobody about. There was a strange smell in the air. We all took some more pictures.

"When we developed the photographs, we were all shocked at what we saw. Nearly every one of them had these strange ghostly lights on them, yet we had used four different cameras-- including one that was digital, so used no film at all."

Jean and Carole were quite shocked by the strange events they experienced during their vacation. I quote the case because I know them to be sensible people who are not prone to fantasy. The notion of a 'time slip" sounds like science fiction, yet there are many well-authenticated examples. Some of the most famous reports have happened at the palace of Versailles near Paris. There, people have suddenly found themselves transported to the time of Marie Antoinette. Remarkably, the scenes these psychic time travellers have described are historically accurate and reveal details about the palace's layout that are only known to the most knowledgeable historians.

This encounter is not the first incident in which paranormal occurrences have happened at Gettysburg. During this bloody battle, the apparition of George Washington appeared to the Confederate troops. It caused a significant retreat and may have given the Union soldiers a victory. At one point, the figure raised his hand, led General Oliver Hunt's soldiers in spontaneous charge down Little Roundtop hill, and fell upon the Rebels. Taken by surprise at such a bold manoeuvre, the Rebels retreated.

Edward Stanton, Secretary of War under Abraham Lincoln, even went so far as to conduct an official investigation of the incident. Today, the park rangers still receive reports of a ghostly man that rides the battlefield on a magnificent white stallion. He wears a tricorn hat and has a luminous aura surrounding him.

Earth Energies, Standing Stones, and Crop Circles

"Whenever a place has had prayers and concentrated desires directed towards it, it forms an electrical vortex that gathers to itself a force, and it is for a time a coherent body that can be felt and used by man. It is around these bodies of force that shrines, temples, and in later days churches are built; they are Cups that receive the Cosmic down-pouring focused on each particular place."
--Dion Fortune

Just as collective thought can create a mind field that imprints itself as a recording onto the atmosphere of an environment, so too, there are certain places where mental energies are magnified. Here, even the emotional state of one individual may leave a lasting imprint. Some parapsychologists claim that certain areas are affected by harmful earth rays and that these places can cause illness, poltergeist activity, and retain negative energies from the past. Some people believe that these places are portals to demonic spirit planes, accounting for why they usually have a history of paranormal and ghostly occurrences. People who live in an area affected by these hostile forces will suffer from a condition called "geopathic stress."

In ancient times, humankind was a nomad who moved from one religious site to another. Today the Aborigines of Australia continue these ancient treks, with each tribe looking after their sacred line that connects the holy centres. These traditions may date to the Stone

Age. At one time, the Aborigine people's knowledge may have been universal, and people around the world would "walk the sacred paths" to connect the energy of the earth. Perhaps such early peoples built the standing stones of places like Stonehenge to canalize the force and act as outlets for this energy. The techniques seem reminiscent of acupuncture, which stimulates and directs the body's vital life force. The standing stones may have served a similar purpose for Earth's life-force.

The ancient monoliths and the pyramids of Egypt would have also acted as amplifiers for these energies. Many of today's geomancers call these concentrations of earth energy "vortices." They are points of power or earth energy linked together by straight lines of energy called "ley lines." An analogy might be that the vortices are acupuncture points and ley lines are the Earth's meridians. These focuses of energy are believed to be very important spiritually as they enhance our consciousness. They are sacred spaces where we can come close to God.

Sacred sites of the ancient world are located at these vortices. In 1921, Alfred Watkins observed that many roads, footpaths, and farm tracks form an impressive network connecting old churches, ancient mounds, and standing stones. In his book *The Old Straight Track*, Watkins named these "ley lines" and argued that these grassy tracks were ancient trade routes. Towards the end of his life, he concluded that ley lines were of religious significance. Others have theorized that these ley lines reveal patterns of triangles between these ancient sites. It is thought that the Indians of the American Southwest and those in Peru and other parts of South America located their cities and the roads between them on vortices and ley lines. And very ancient sites such as Stonehenge, the Great Pyramid, and Glastonbury Tor in the UK are believed to conform to these patterns. The ideas were elaborated on by the author Guy Underwood who claimed that these ancient sites were founded on underground streams that somehow connected to the energies of the earth. Dowsing revealed that this earth energy was some kind of spiralling magnetic force. The author John Mitchell expanded these ideas further, claiming that the crossing points of these ley lines (called nodes) are often associated with UFO sightings and paranormal activity.

It may also be the case that earth energies are responsible for crop circles around the world. Many of these are the work of pranksters, but others may be caused by earth energy, or Mother Gaia's energy, streaming out of the earth. Some have appeared within a few miles of my home at places I would consider being high in energy. Indeed, those I meet who have a keen interest in these things claim to feel the energy in these places. The patterns crop circles form is undoubtedly impressive, but I am yet to be convinced that they are the work of extraterrestrial intelligence.

Sick Buildings

"Buildings, too, are children of Earth and Sun."
--FRANK LLOYD WRIGHT

I remember an occasion when sitting by a lake, I became aware of an energy that appeared to flow from the trees in the distance, over the lake, and into a spiral pattern near where I was standing. This phenomenon was something I could see with my everyday perceptions, and it took me entirely by surprise. It looked like the glossy smudged spirals you see if you pour boiling water into a cold bath. I now understood that chi energy could move across an environment and absorb vibrations as it flowed over different areas. In this case, the power it was picking up from the lake felt restorative and uplifting. I could now see this happening with my own eyes. Clearly--for me at least--earth energy is a reality.

As energy moves over an environment, it absorbs the vibrations of the things it encounters. In this way, the energy influencing us can be beneficial or harmful. This 'chi energy' is one of the main ideas behind the Chinese art of Feng Shui, which I will touch upon in due course. However, there are also forces acting upon us from below the ground, rising upward from beneath the earth. The combination of the radiating earth energies and the flowing earth energies on our planet's surface has a significant influence on an environment's wholesomeness.

Earth energies and ley lines can also have a sinister side. When the energy from a ley line passes through decaying matter such as a city dump, a polluted river, or a graveyard, it picks up the negative influences it encounters. The energy becomes what geomancers call a "black stream." Similarly, energy moving beneath the earth may encounter underground water streams, geological fissures, and fault lines that interfere with it. This, too, can cause a "black stream" of earth energy. Someone living or sleeping in these areas may become ill or emotionally disturbed by these influences. Many practitioners believe that "black streams" can even cause cancer.

The Earth behaves like a massive electromagnet with many geo-electromagnetic field lines crossing its surface and rising through the earth. This natural radiation is distorted by other electromagnetic fields, subterranean running water, certain mineral concentrations, fault lines, underground caves, cosmic radiation, and artificially created electromagnetic fields.

A person who is adversely affected by these negative earth rays suffers from what we call "geopathic stress." They can lose physical strength, energy, emotional stability, and happiness.

Geopathic Stress

"If you have a black spiral of telluric energies in your bed, you will be susceptible to geopathic stress and ill-health. An unhealthy ley line (a stream of individual waves) radiates into the spiral."
--David R. Cowan, author of *Safe As Houses*

I have worked with Ken Nielsen, one of the world's leading experts in geopathic stress. Ken runs an organization called Geomack, whose business is to clear environments affected by geopathic stress, primarily buildings. Ken claims that geopathic stress can seriously affect specific settings. "The indoor environment can vary greatly from building to building. One may have the most relaxing, well-balanced, and warm feeling. Another may have a feeling of discomfort and seem cold and unpleasant. We often ignore the warning we get of feeling a strange reaction to certain houses or buildings time after time until we lose our ability to sense these signals at all. The gradual effect on people (or some animals and plants) can lead to slow deterioration in health in individuals susceptible to such stress. Any illness or ailment likely seems to worsen during periods of heavy rain or at the full moon. We spend approximately one-third of our lives in bed! Since we spend such a large amount of time in one location, it is especially crucial there to be free of harmful energy fields."

Ken's remedy for a building affected by geopathic stress is to supply a particular machine that utilizes the building's electrical wiring to influence the earth rays. Ken has many testimonials from worthy people who claim that their symptoms disappear after using Ken's "Energia" machines. I have no idea how they work, so I cannot comment, but there are undoubtedly other remedies that can be used to protect your environment from harmful earth rays. (More details about the Energia can be found on Ken's website www.geomack.com .)

The first step is to ascertain whether damaging earth rays do affect your environment. Since there is, unfortunately, no machine that can measure earth rays, diagnosis is usually done by dowsing. One of the most straightforward techniques employed by Ken Nielsen uses a semicircle divided into degrees--like the protractor you may have used at school. In the middle, at the point where you would find 90 degrees on a protractor, the value is given as zero. To the right of this, the numerals run from plus 1 to plus 20. To the left, the numbers run from minus one to minus 20.

A pendulum is now held over the semicircle at the zero line and allowed to swing as the dowser thinks about the environment or room he wants to diagnose. The swing may remain at the zero line or now swing towards the positive or negative numbers. If the swing is in the positive area, then the geopathic energy in the environment of okay. If it swings to the negative numbers on the left, the site is affected by geopathic stress. A minus one would be acceptable, but a minus twenty would be a potentially dangerous environment.

Of course, many dowsing techniques can be applied to identify areas affected by geopathic stress. If you would like more details, I have posted some of the main techniques on my website (www.psychics.co.uk)

Once the area affected by geopathic stress is identified, several remedies are available to help negate the negative energy. The first thing to do is usually to change the place you sleep. Sleeping over a "black stream" is very harmful, so the bed (or bedroom) may have to be moved. It is essential to identify the best position in the house to place the bed.

Some practitioners protect the bed by placing materials beneath it to shield you from negative earth rays. Sheet glass or a mirror (face down) placed beneath the bed are claimed to reflect negative rays. A sheet of toughened glass, such as an old car windscreen, is effective. Similarly, iron or corrugated iron beneath the bed may help to protect you. Putting two sheets head to head under the bed will also work, but they must be overlapping; otherwise, noxious energy will immediately rise vertically through the join between them. The entire area of the person(s) to be protected must be covered, with the possible exception of the feet and legs.

Crystals are also considered an effective remedy for removing geopathic stress. Dowsing techniques can identify areas where energies are blocked and find the points which can be worked on with earth acupuncture techniques. For this, crystals are placed or buried in strategic places to enable earth energy to flow better. In most cases, clear quartz crystals can be used as these are powerful amplifiers of energy. If placed where the energy is negative, they will lift the energy in this affected area. Other crystals will bring different powers to bear on the environment. For example, rose quartz and amethyst have healing properties and may be used to calm the energy in a disturbed area. In particular, they help change the course of a ley line. For example, the crystal is "charged" by the practitioner by holding it in their hands and making a sincere request. They may say something such as, "May this crystal move the negative ley line." Once the request is complete, the area is dowsed, and the crystal then placed in the most promising spot. Additional techniques involve burying lengths of copper wire in areas surrounding a building to deflect negative earth energy.

Specific crystals increase the energies that the individual needs. For example, if you feel depressed, the dowser may place tourmaline, coral or pyrite to lift and calm the energy. Crystals and gemstones have many different functions. They secure an environment from negativity and make specific enhancements to the energies.

Using Crystals, Gemstones and Metals

Every discolouration of the stone, Every accidental crack or dent,
Seems a water-course or an avalanche, Or lofty slope where it still snows
--**W. B. YEATS** (from *Lapis Lazuli*)

Current interest in the healing and protective power of crystals can be traced to some writings about American psychic Edgar Cayce and many scattered references to crystals in his readings. Edgar Cayce (1877-1945) was one of the most influential psychics of all time. When he died, he left behind a unique resource; complete transcripts of over 1600 readings given in the last decades of his life to hundreds of people who came to him for help and advice. Cayce considered lapis lazuli to be one of the most important stones for protection. While in a trance, he is recorded as saying, "… the lapis ligurius would bring much that will act in a manner as would be termed a protective influence if kept about the entity" (1931-1 M.20 born 9/11/19). Lapis Lazuli is the most frequently mentioned gem material in the Cayce readings and can have many spiritual qualities. Cayce speaks of how the high electrical vibration of this gem material can strengthen and aid the individual and create a better relationship between the mental and spiritual selves. It is also said to bring live vitality and healing. (Cayce also recommended beryl and scarab for their protective qualities)

It is interesting to note that the ancient cultures of India also believe that adverse influences can be countered in some instances by wearing certain gems, stones or metals. The Indian master Yogananda received these interesting words of advice from his own master Sri Yukteswar:

"Just as a house may be fitted with a copper rod to absorb the shock of lightening, so the bodily temple can be protected in certain ways.

Electrical and magnetic radiations are ceaselessly circulating in the universe; they affect man's body for good and ill. Ages ago, our rishis pondered the problem of combating the adverse effects of subtle cosmic influences. The sages discovered that pure metals emit an astral light, which is powerfully counteractive to the planets' negative pulls. Certain plant combinations were also found helpful. Most effective of all are faultless jewels of not less than two carats.

The practical preventative uses of astrology have seldom been seriously studied outside of India. One little-known fact is that the proper jewels, metals and plant preparations are valueless unless the required weight secured and unless the remedial agent is worn next to the skin.

For general purposes, I counsel the use of an armlet made of gold, silver, and copper. But for a specific purpose, I want you to get one of silver and lead."

In recent years, these ideas have resurfaced. I am in contact with many people who experiment with materials' properties, trying to find ways to use as protection from not only earth energies but also vibrations and rays projected from machinery and domestic appliances. Computers and mobile phones are said to be particularly dangerous to our health. A colleague of mine, who experiments with Kirlian photography, has found that the aura appears shattered if photographed while using a mobile phone or computer. I feel that further study is necessary in order to rule out whether it is the equipment itself being influenced by the pulses from a mobile phone. Nonetheless, the initial results are impressive. Findings indicate that one of the best protective materials against this type of influence is black tourmaline. It appears to safeguard the aura.

Other Protective Devices

Some practitioners use leaves, flowers, shells, tree and plant essences, and other natural objects to work on the energy in addition to crystals, gems, and metals. Earth acupuncture is also the perfect complement to space healing. After identifying negativity areas, a space healer may use offerings of flowers, candles, incense, and holy water and use them to create a better ambience in a room. At my spiritual circle, we sometimes clear the space by ringing a Balinese temple bell in each corner of the room. If a bell is not available, clapping at "stagnant" areas, such as corners or in spaces below tables, will lift the energy in these places. After using sound, we burn frankincense in a special burner and swing it into the appropriate areas. We then play relaxing music and arrange the lighting so that the environment is thoroughly cleansed and maintains harmony. When this is done in advance of a spiritual circle or demonstration of mediumship, we notice a definite improvement in the room's energies.

Fragrance has been used for centuries as a means of clearing negative energy. The most popular today are cedar wood, pine, and juniper. In Arabia, frankincense is burned to clear a house of bad spirits. Juniper and rosemary served the same purpose in Mediaeval Europe. Native Americans also burned juniper to remove evil spirits, whereas the aroma of burning sweet-grass or sage purifies the energies and attracts benign spirits. Similarly, in Tibet, juniper is offered to good spirits, and in the Chinese Feng Shui spirit-placating rite of *tun fu*, incense is used.

In a similar vein, some scented oils are considered to protect an individual from negative vibrations. For example, civit is a rich, musk-like fragrance that can be rubbed onto the hands or used to anoint the feet. Cyclamen is supposed to strengthen men and protect families. Myrrh, which the Magi brought to the baby Jesus, is an ancient protection of the Nature Deities. Many people today rub this oil into their foreheads as a protection against evil. Similarly, oak moss, when rubbed around a doorway, is said to prevent evil from entering, and it will bring harmony to the home or workplace.

Other protective oils include sandalwood, which guards a person working with clairvoyance and safeguards them from interference from hostile elementals or mischievous nature spirits. Similarly, verbena added to a bath will remove negativity. A little verbena oil added to a black candle will fill a room with a sense of safety and protection. Similarly, wormwood can be worn for protection or added to a "reversing candle." These half red/half black candles are claimed to "turn any situation around," making generators of trouble see the error of their ways.

Many of these fragrances are used alongside crystals and other techniques described above to improve the positive energy in an environment.

Nature Spirits and Faeries

"This we know: The Earth does not belong to man; man belongs to the Earth. This we know. All things are united like the blood, which unites one family. All things are connected. Whatever befalls the Earth befalls the sons of the Earth. Man did not weave the web of life; he is merely a strand in it. Whatever he does to the web he does to himself."
--Chief Seattle

Most fragrances are associated with a flower, tree, or plant and tradition has it that connected with each of these is a protective spirit. Usually called elementals, they may include nature spirits, faeries, devas, pixies, elves, etc. Today we think of fairies as sweet little creatures with gossamer wings, but they were beings to be feared and avoided in the past. The Irish poet Yeats called them the "gods of the earth" and believed that they "have no inherent form but changed according to their whim, or the mind that sees them."

Could some places be influenced by invisible spirits that can occasionally manifest spirits to people who are open to them? Indeed, many people believe that fairies can be our protective helpers--or may be something we need protection from. The Pygmy Theory attests that fairies are a folk memory of a people who did exist and inhabited the Earth long ago. Today, we see them as ghostlike images at places where the natural earth energy is intense.

It may be that fairies and other elemental beings are spirits at an early stage of evolution existing somewhere between human and animal form. Similarly, they could be like the thought-forms that we discussed earlier--possibly created by centuries of fear and superstition. The psychologist Carl Jung explained that they are symbols from the unconscious.

Since Sir Arthur Conan Doyle's somewhat naïve acceptance of some fake fairy photographs, this has become a bit of a no-go area for Spiritualists! Nonetheless, I recall standing near a well on an ancient British ley line site and seeing all around me tiny creatures of light. My Irish friend, who had been walking with me, saw them simultaneously and immediately accepted them as fairy lights. They were not an optical effect, coming from rubbing the eyes, and they could not have been fireflies. But what is most puzzling is that moments before seeing them, we had been immersed in a conversation as we walked about whether fairies exist or not. Certainly, the experience, for my friend and me at least, gave credence to their reality.

A great many superstitions surround the appeasement of fairies. For example, in many parts of Europe, the spilling of milk was considered good luck, as it provided food for the good fairies that scurried about on the ground. Paying homage to the fairies in this way would buy their protection against evil spirits or bad luck. Certain times of year are associated with fairies, too. For example, the first of May is regarded as a special time in the pagan calendar. On this day, you should keep your eye on the clock, for until noon, the power of the fairies is at its strongest. Only after the sun sets in the evening, and the official end of the traditional May Day festival, are we safe from fairy mischief!

One of the greatest fears associated with fairies was that they could steal babies that had not been baptized. To avoid this, concerned parents must tie up a little bit of salt in the baby's dress before laying it down to sleep. Mobiles designed to hang over a baby's bed were made of scissors! Hanging like the sword of Damocles, they were said to protect the child from fairies. Covering the child with an article of clothing belonging to the father served the same purpose, however. (My socks can keep away the evilest of spirits!) Folklore says that adults should use fire to protect themselves from fairy magic because only humans have the power to overcome and control the flames. The most certain protection technique is to make a ring of fire around a child's cradle, so fairies have no power to harm the child. I do not, however, recommend this technique as it may do the baby great harm. At the least, I have found that the ceilings tend to get a little sooty.

Popular today are the flower fairies that are seen on greeting cards and the like. Many people believe that certain associated flowers can have a protective influence. For example, a lavender flower helps us contact the fairies, whereas rosemary gives protection from dangerous ones. The gardenia flower's fairy spirits are said to protect loved ones and children, and the snapdragon fairies bring protection from deceit and curses. Hold these flowers secretly in your hand, and others will see you as gracious and fascinating.

Similarly, trees have protective fairy spirits that can be summoned in times of need. The most sacred tree of all is the hawthorn, the sacred tree of the fairies. Its spirit knows protection as well as growth and fertility. Other protection fairies are associated with the alder, which protects clairvoyants working with scrying; the cedar brings calm and balance, and spruce growing in your backyard will protect the family while sleeping. Many people still take fairies seriously, calling upon them for help or for special magical powers. For most people today, fairies are no longer the frightening elementals associated with particular sacred sites and earth energy. Instead, they have become benign, silly things, as depicted in Disney's illustrations, Arthur Rackham, Henry Hall Pickersgill and Richard Dadd. Perhaps our modern scepticism, past superstition, and romantic notions blind us to a fascinating aspect of nature that is worthy of proper investigation.

Feng Shui

"Use symbols appropriate to your background and culture. For instance, Santa Claus is a symbol of abundance too! You can use that."
--LILLIAN TOO (Feng Shui Master)

We've discussed how specific environments lift your spirits while others drain you and how this may be caused by earth energies or the vibrations resonating in a place from previous occupants. The Chinese have been aware of these effects for centuries. To combat these negative energies, they developed the art of Feng Shui. The protection of Feng Shui comes from deliberately creating energies in your surroundings that will continually increase and support your sense of well-being, in this way protecting your soul from negative influences.

What we have called "earth energy" corresponds to the effect of Chi energy in Feng Shui. "Earth energy" and "chi energy" are, similarly, the life force at work. It is not only present in all living things but moves about the planet. This Chi energy is everywhere and may manifest itself with positive and negative aspects. You will sense its positive aspect when a place "feels right." When you purchase a property, this feeling suggests that the energy of the property may be in harmony with your dreams and desires. The Chinese believe that this will protect you from bad luck and attract good fortune into your life.

People who complain of geopathic stress or believe they live in an environment with no positive chi also claim that they are beset with bad luck. According to the ancient Chinese, good fortune is not a result of chance but created by the Chi energy all around us. Think of chi as a life force that moves, like a wind, through the environment. It also has the qualities of water, for it absorbs and releases the vibrations given out by the things it comes in contact with. The chi around you at this moment may be full of positive influences that will bring you luck or filled with stagnant influences which will draw misfortune to you. Besides, this chi energy can influence your wealth, health, relationships, and every single aspect of your life. Negative chi can harm our lives' quality, but good chi will make us healthy and happy. Getting the chi in an environment right can therefore act as robust protection for the soul.

Fortunately, we need not be at the mercy of bad chi. We can improve our lives by influencing chi energy so that it continually works in our favour. The art of enhancing these energies is Feng Shui, translated literally "Wind and Water." It was a secret art reserved for the fortunate ruling class who could afford to employ a Feng Shui master to manage their environment in antiquity. The extremely ancient system dates back over 5,000 years. Today, the "secrets of the dragon's cosmic breath" –as the sages described it--are finally being revealed to us in the west. Now we can all use Feng Shui to live in harmony with our environment and draw upon the subtle energies that will nurture our health, wealth, and happiness.

A Simple Overview of Feng Shui

The Chinese tell us that all life on this planet is animated by the life force called chi. It is in everything. It is universal. It is in us and all around us. It is in the flowing rivers, the ascending mountains, the wide plains, our cities and our homes, and it influences our prosperity, health, love, and happiness.

Chi flows through everything just as we are surrounded by the invisible energies of electricity, microwaves, radio, and TV signals, so chi energy also permeates our world.

In its most positive form, it is called Sheng Chi, and where it is concentrated, plants flourish, animals flourish, and we flourish. It never moves fast, and it can accumulate in the environment and even within our bodies. The best place for chi to accumulate is where the air is fresh, and water flows slowly and sinuously. The flow of water and of chi is an integral part of Feng Shui. For example, many of the world's great cities, such as Hong Kong, London, Paris, and San Francisco, are built on sheltered harbours or slow-flowing rivers. Not only are these sites practical for shipping, but they are places where chi is greatest. Some of these cities are particularly blessed because they have water access at the front and are protected in the rear by mountains. Hong Kong is positioned between the South China Sea and the Central mountains of China; New York between the Appalachians and the Atlantic; and London between the Chilterns and the River Thames. The water and wind elements of chi energy in these locations are perfectly balanced and encourage life and stimulate trade.

Sheng Chi brings good fortune and is described as clean, vibrant, and energetic. However, it should not be allowed to gather great speed, or it will become harmful. A widespread Feng Shui technique is to use water as a means to control the flow of chi. When chi encounters water, it settles, so water can be used to accumulate Sheng chi. If a water feature, such as a fountain, for example, is placed in an auspicious position near a home, it will bring good luck to the front door.

Chi can also stagnate or be dissipated quickly. Where it stagnates and forms backwaters, the life force will be reduced. The Chinese name for this manifestation of chi is Shar chi. Life in areas affected by Shar chi gradually wither away. In other places, chi rushes past and cannot accumulate. Beside fast-moving rivers or roads, for example, good chi energy does not have time to gather, so there is no beneficial effect on life in these areas. Unpleasant shapes and form can increase hostile chi. Sharp edges, massive structures, and angular shapes can increase this negative energy, usually called "poison arrows" by most schools.

Within nature and in our home environment, beneficial chi is enhanced when it echoes nature's gentle flowing curves.

Harmonizing with Positive Energy

"That which exists through itself is called the Tao."
The Secret of the Golden Flower

There is no space here to explain all of Feng Shui's aspects and how it is used to improve and protect your environment. However, it is worth considering the spiritual part that many books about the subject often leave out. Feng Shui is about much more than interior design. It has a spiritual dimension. You may have heard of the word Tao (pronounced "Daoe"). Tao is an important aspect of Feng Shui. It literally translates as "the way." Many Feng Shui principles come from this ancient Chinese nature religion of Taoism. The Chinese say that everything is the Tao, and from it comes everything we can know.

We do not have a word in English that adequately describes Tao. Perhaps the easiest way to understand it is as being the quintessence of all things: the fundamental inspiration from which everything flows. Walk in harmony with the Tao, and you are on the right path and at one with the life force. The spiritual objective of Feng Shui is to conform our lives to the Tao and see the ordered pathway through all situations. It is like the golden thread that Theseus used to find his way through the Minotaur's labyrinth, or perhaps described as the "right way" in any given situation. It's "going with the flow." A person in harmony with the Tao is protected from negative energy and evil influences because he or she is at one with the source of life itself.

Taoist philosophers tell us that the universe is divided into two aspects. They called these forces yin and yang. Material reality is yin, as yin covers all things tangible--things that can be held. Yin is a feminine force and means earth or matter. It is symbolized by a square and is black. Yin is associated with night, stillness, down, inner, winter, and the north. Conversely, yang is the intangible aspect of creation represented by heaven. Its symbol is a circle, and it is considered masculine. It is white, and associated with day, activity, up, outer, summer, and the south.

Yin and Yang are fundamental to Chinese philosophy. They are not seen as opposing forces but as complimentary, altering and moving each other in an eternal change process. Their interaction gives rise to all things. In the Chinese book called the *I Ching*, the ancient sages studied yin and yang's interaction in nature and devised an oracle system that could be applied to all situations. In the written form, they represented yang with a straight line and yin with a broken one. Groups of three of any of these lines are called trigrams. Each represents a different quality and direction. In all, eight trigrams are possible. When laid out in an octagon form, the Ba-gua --known as the Great symbol--give the qualities of each compass direction used in Feng Shui.

The primary objective of Feng Shui is to balance the energies of yin and yang and align the practitioner with the Tao. When we do this, we are not only spiritually protected but draw good health, harmony, and good fortune into our orbit. Similar principles underlie Chinese medicine, yoga, acupuncture, martial arts, Tai Chi, art, music, alchemy, and meditation. When the soul is in harmony with the Tao, it is perfectly protected.

Improving Energy with Feng Shui

Feng Shui is part practical and part intuitive. Indeed, the great Feng Shui masters are proficient in both aspects of this art. Be in tune with your feelings and observant of your surroundings. Be aware of both your outer and inner environments and how they relate to each other. Do your moods change with your surroundings? Observing your own reactions and moods and the reactions and behavior of others will give you important insights into the chi's nature in a particular environment. It takes a great deal of study and practice to master Feng Shui, but there are a few simple remedies you can apply to combat negative energy in your environment.

Remove clutter

Clutter and mess are a terrible influence upon the smooth flowing of chi. A good friend and Feng Shui practitioner points out that it is beneficial always to apply the three C's. That is, Constantly Clear Clutter. Clutter disrupts good chi. And this also applies to the places that are "out of sight, out of mind," such as drawers, attics, computer files, and even the glove compartment of your car.

Chi flows around your home, within your car, and even within the electronics of a computer. If it has to travel through the clutter, the influences upon your life will never be focused. A pattern of indecision and disorganization will be the primary influence around you. So get rid of all clutter everywhere. You want your living spaces to flow with good chi. Ignore this principle, and the areas of your life that correspond to your messy areas will be correspondingly disturbed. For example, clutter left in the career area, which is the north, may result in a trashed business plan. Or leave rubbish in the northeast, the study location, and you may be disappointed by an exam result.

Dust, dirt, stains, rust, and so on also have the same harmful effect upon the chi entering your living space. Even blemished mirrors should be replaced so that the reflection is not adversely affected. So the first golden rule for a good Feng Shui environment is simply to make sure everything is clean, tidy, and orderly. This will allow protective energy to surround you and help clear any negativity.

Visit places high in naturally occurring Chi

You may have noticed that flat open spaces have a completely different energy level to deep valleys, mountain ranges, or built-up areas. Early Feng Shui patriarchs observed how quick-moving shallow streams and rivers disperse chi, as do mountains and hills that are exposed to high winds. They also discovered that clear pools, lakes, and low-lying valleys accumulate chi. These are places of great energy and promote inner harmony, peace, and quiet. The power in the landscape will help restore you and remove any negative energy that has polluted your aura.

Since ancient times, Feng Shui practitioners have recognized that certain places accumulate chi and are auspicious places to live. Using a special compass called the lo p'an they found that the nature of the chi energy changes from direction to direction. By pinpointing where the chi flows most favourably, Feng Shui practitioners can identify the best sites to locate homes, businesses, and industries. This particular technique is called "tapping the veins of the dragon." Just as with the examples given about ley lines and crop circles, Feng Shui can help us identify places with protective energy.

Identify settings that have gentle natural curves

Angular shapes are considered significantly harmful in the art of Feng Shui. Sharp corners of one building pointing at another are likened to a knife cutting into the threatened building occupants' well-being and slicing through their good fortune. It is particularly bad if the corner points to the all-important entrance to the building. The areas that are most likely to have a protective quality have gentle curves. These are the places you may use for rest and meditation.

Take a few moments to think about your own home or business. How is it positioned? How do the roads approach it? Is the house directly approached by roads, as if being attacked by arrows? Or does the road curve gently, with the house on the inside curve. What about the path to your front door? Is this a frontal attack, or does the path sweep in gently from the side? Is there a beneficial water source, such as a garden pond, in an area that may accumulate chi? What about the angles of other buildings facing your home: do they "cut" into it--or harmonize with it? These are all problem areas that may give you a feeling of being under a psychic attack. To discover other techniques to protect your environment, you may want to study Feng Shui in more detail.

Buy a home in an auspicious area if possible

In Feng Shui terms, every room in your house relates to an aspect of your life quality. It is therefore essential to keep each area in a good state. For example, a negative influence created by dust and dirt in the northern part of your home will affect the corresponding sphere of influence, which in this case is your career.

Within the home, the state of the front door is also of utmost importance. It is regarded as the mouth of the house through which chi enters; therefore, it should be kept in a good state of repair. The nature of the energy that enters from the front door can affect the home.

On New Year's Eve, my grandmother used to open the back door to let out the old and open the front door to let in the new. This is an ancient western tradition that continues to this day. My grandmother knew nothing about Feng Shui, but, in essence, she was employing its principles. The forces that come in through the front door affect the house and the fortunes of the individuals living within it. A house that faces a cemetery, industrial smokestack, electrical tower, or a slaughterhouse, for example, will be affected by the negative qualities of the area in front of it. The chi entering your home picks up residual energies from whatever it passes, like a smell being carried on the wind.

If your house faces a cemetery, the in-flowing chi will pick up the grief; from a slaughterhouse, it will carry pain; and from a dump or trash heap, it will carry decay. But, if your entrance faces a beautiful scene or landscape, the chi entering your home will be saturated with positive and uplifting vibrations. Location, location, location! The real estate agents are right when they tout location as one of the most important factors when buying a home or business premises. The Chinese would say that it is *the most* important factor.

Dress appropriately

Even your clothes can affect the chi you attract. Lost buttons, dirt, stains, and faded colours all affect your personal chi. They disrupt your chi and therefore affect your attitude and good fortune. A positive attitude to life is also beneficial and will in itself increase your personal chi and the chi that flows through your body. However, a positive attitude requires constant effort to maintain, but it becomes more spontaneous if you've removed any obstacle that blocks good chi from coming to you. By keeping things in good order, you protect yourself from negative influences and attract beneficial chi that will bring to you deserved abundance of health, wealth, and happiness.

Surround yourself with things high-chi

Chi flows through the body and is the basis of Chinese medicine. For example, acupuncture redirects the flow of chi along the body's meridians and so promotes better health, Chinese herbalism is designed to work with chi, and the martial arts, such as Kung Fu, stimulate the body's latent chi energy so that the practitioners can perform super-human acts of strength. Likewise, your health will be influenced for the better by applying Feng Shui principles, such as activating the eastern sector of your home, which governs health. This is achieved by placing a healthy plant, particularly one with round leaves, in this area. A plant belongs to the wood element, which in turn corresponds with the east direction. As the plant thrives, so will you. In addition, think about the chi in your food and drink. Fresh fruit, for example, is alive with chi energy, which acts upon your body as a healing force.

Feng Shui and relationships

Feng Shui can also be used to improve relationships. It helps us interact with people because our improved outlook will make other people's perception of us more positive. Also, it improves family relationships and may attract new people into our lives. There are special Feng Shui formulas to target whatever relationship aspect of your life you may want to improve: with your children, parents, friends, or partner. You can even use it to influence your boss. In the same way, targeting Feng Shui in relationships can give you a better rapport at work to help you with career advancement.

Here's something to try, designed to attract helpful friends. Put the telephone in the northeast area of your home, office, or desk, as this direction relates to helpful people and mentors. It would help if the telephone were of metallic colours, such as grey; metal is the northeast element. If you are eager to increase a bond with your partner, hang a happy photograph of you both together in the southwest area of your home. The southwest direction relates to romantic happiness.

Attract good luck

The Chinese use Feng Shui mainly to improve wealth and prosperity. Once this area of life is sorted out, they feel it is much easier to improve all other concerns. The accumulation and subtle effect of chi will influence the physical plane, creating increased business opportunities and a corresponding increase in wealth. Next time you go into a Chinese restaurant, look at how they use Feng Shui to attract wealth. You will notice statues or figures representing long life, fertility, and abundance. And you will probably see the Chinese character for "great good fortune doubled" hung in a frame; I once saw it woven into the carpet.

The Chinese will put a fish tank near the cash register because water accumulates chi, and, of course, the till is their most important wealth area. Feng Shui's rules recommend that an aquarium-- preferably round (remember sharp edges project "cutting" chi which can be harmful)--should be kept in the southeast corner and must be large enough to contain nine healthy goldfish. Only one of these fish should be of the black variety. The flickering light from the tank signifies active turnover, thereby increasing sales. Also, fish is a symbol of abundance. They are also good to keep in a pond and will help accumulate and circulate chi. Again, the rule is that they should be in multiples of nine. For a small tank, three gold and two black are recommended.

Use positive symbolism around the home

The use of symbolism will influence your environment. In the late nineteen seventies, it became fashionable in the UK to hang prints of paintings of wide-eyed, crying children on the wall. Their imagery was sentiment taken to the extreme. You can still buy pictures like this.

But some strange eerie stories started to appear in the press about these pictures. According to the reporters, houses that hung a particular picture of a wide-eyed, crying boy would burn to the ground. The homes would be decimated, but the image of the boy would remain completely unscathed.

We still do not know what was behind these paranormal events, but some Feng Shui consultants have argued that the picture was so chi negative that it was actually causing the disasters. Badly chosen imagery such as this can bring misfortune to the home and is, in itself, depressing. It is better to choose uplifting imagery: positive symbols, pictures, or photographs that are a tribute to nature. These attract favourable chi.

Feng Shui employs the symbols used in ancient China, such as the black turtle, crimson phoenix, green dragon, and white tiger. Other examples of the use of potent symbols of good fortune include a statue of a laughing Buddha (fortunate if placed in a foyer, but not in the dining room). Shells are lucky for travel, in particular, the conch shell or those shaped like it. Like the goldfish, Japanese carp or the expensive arrowana fish are considered lucky. With its round leaves and no thorns, the jade plant is the perfect plant to attract wealth, particularly when placed in the money area--the southeast. The deer is also considered a fortunate symbol of health, and the crane is one of the most beautiful symbols of longevity. A representation of the phoenix or a rooster or a flamingo can be used to enhance your fame and fortune area, which is the south. You may not feel comfortable because of western superstition, having peacock feathers in the house; many people consider them to be "the evil eye." But in China, peacocks and their feathers are a symbol of great good luck.

If you do choose western symbolism, think very carefully about its meaning and its benefit, or harm will become apparent. Analyze the intrinsic meaning of any image, picture, statue, or object you bring into your environment. Think carefully about what its shape, form, and symbolism mean and whether these qualities will be helpful. For instance, dried flowers and dead wood have been associated with death in the form of ornamental branches, so the chi is negative. Surround yourself with uplifting imagery.

You can also use other techniques to activate the chi in your environment. Things that pleasantly attract your senses will attract positive chi; incense and fragrances, for instance, improve the atmosphere. Candles and up-lighting lift the chi levels, especially in the south and southwest, your fame and romantic areas. Chandeliers are considered very useful chi stimulators. Consider also using pleasant sounds such as wind chimes, water and gentle music, which encourage chi. Moving objects, such as mobiles, also activate chi, as do electrically powered items such as TV's, stereos and computers.

Many people worry that they cannot apply Feng Shui in their

homes or workplace because it requires either a vast amount of personal knowledge about the subject or an enormous amount of money to pay for a reputable practitioner. Many of Feng Shui rules are common sense, and it is easy to use these simple methods to create a setting that nurtures your positive energy and protects your soul from environmental negativity.

4 ECLIPSED SOULS

"A ruffled mind makes a restless pillow."
--CHARLOTTE BRONTE

True reports about ghosts, ghouls, and spirits are a recurring theme in day-to-day correspondence generated by my media exposure. From the incoming mail, it is clear that a surprising number of people claim to have had paranormal experiences, and many ask for help in dealing with malevolent spiritual forces. One widespread problem seems to be spirit attacks while people sleep. The sinister entity may grab the sleeper by the throat, sit on their chest, and in some instances sexually abuse them.

Could it be that a large sector of the population is under attack by demons? Indeed, some of the letters I have received indicate that this is happening: "I awoke one morning and realized that my body was completely paralyzed," writes one reader. "I couldn't move a muscle. Something was in the room, and walked across the bed. I tried to scream, but only a slight noise came from my throat. Whoever or whatever was in my room then disappeared. Unfortunately, I have been getting this horrible paralysis for about two months now. The last time it happened, I managed to open my eyes but still could not move my body."

This person is probably suffering from what psychologists call "sleep paralysis." Recent surveys suggest that it affects between 25 to 30 per cent of the population. People also frequently report feeling a "presence" that is often described as hateful, threatening, or evil. An intense sense of dread and terror is pervasive. Sometimes the "entity" may attack by strangling the sleeper and exerting crushing pressure on the chest. It is caused when the back of the brain comes to consciousness before the rest of the body "wakes up." This is more likely to happen if you are overtired. Doctors also advise that it is best to sleep on your side and not on your back, which can trigger the condition.

If you find yourself in the midst of a sleep-paralysis episode, you might try a traditional method for overcoming the paralysis by attempting to move your fingers or toes, or even your tongue. A number of people have suggested rapidly moving one's eyes back and forth as a way of bringing a bout of SP to an end. As it is possible to have multiple episodes in a single night, it may help to get up briefly and move around after any such episode before trying to sleep again.

In medieval times, people believed in the incubus, a lascivious male demon who possessed mortal women as they slept. He was responsible for the birth of demons, witches, and deformed children. According to one legend, the incubus and his female counterpart, the succubus, were fallen, angels. In medieval European folklore, it is said that female demons may visit men in their sleep to lie with them in ghostly sexual intercourse. The man who succumbs to a succubus will not awaken from sleep. Other folklore speaks of Chinese Fox spirits, East European vampires, an Old Hag myth, and even Eskimo spirits, all including the theme of a person waking up, unable to move, and sensing a presence.

Recent theories claim that these sexual attacks are also the result of sleep paralysis. As we know from Freud, a great deal of dream content is sexual. Some psychologists claim that penile and clitoral erections in REM (dreaming) sleep demonstrates the validity of Freud's insights about the primacy of sex. Also, the asphyxiation that accompanies this syndrome may cause sexual excitement. It is conceivable that many of the sexual attacks these people describe may be simply a vivid waking nightmare with a sexual undertone that occurs during a bout of sleep paralysis. Similarly, psychologists have explained that sleep paralysis may be at the root of cases of people who believe that aliens have abducted them. Often such claims begin with a report of someone waking up, terrified, feeling a presence, unable to move, may include sexual "experiments," and often include waking-dream type hallucinations.

A good night's sleep is essential for a healthy body, mind, and soul. Many of our troubles arise because of over-tiredness that in turn, creates emotional vulnerability and intellectual weakness. In some of my other books, I have explained how to establish positive sleep patterns and prepare an inviolate area where dreams can safely occur. The most common cause of a bad night's sleep and nightmares is mental over-stimulation before bedtime. It is, therefore, essential to prepare your mind for sleep. Avoid watching violent films on TV just before bedtime. Instead, do something restful, such as listening to music or reading something light.

A light snack of foods that are high in tryptophan will also help you sleep. These include eggs, meat nuts, beans, fish, and cheese. Similarly, foods high in carbohydrates help you to sleep, such as cereals, milk, cakes, spaghetti, and honey. Limited consumption of high-fat foods can also help sleep. But it is most important to let go of negative thoughts and fill your mind with positive imagery. You may think of happy events from the past or visualize beautiful places you know. This will create positive thoughts that will keep nightmares away. As I prepare to fall asleep, one of my personal favourites is to imagine that I am being bathed in twinkling golden lights that fall from above. Each one is a spark of energy that carries with it a special blessing to encourage inner peace and wellbeing.

Real Attacks

"I don't believe in ghosts, but I've been afraid of them all my life."
--**Charles A. Dana** (1819-1897).

There are cases in my files of people who appear to have undergone paranormal attacks as they slept. A prison inmate, for example, wrote, "The last time it happened, I was tossing and turning and trying to get to sleep when a strange dark power pulled me off the bed and pushed me against the wall. My cellmate screamed when he saw what was happening." Similarly, an old lady relayed, "I am terrified at night as I believe that a ghost or spirit is menacing me. If I awake during the night, I see what I would call "smoke" in my room. One night my husband and I saw the harrowing sight of my bedclothes being slowly pulled off the bed. But the last straw was when I felt "it" move to the side of the bed and poke me hard in the arm. I prayed out loud but it wouldn't go away."

Other case files are reports of people who have been attacked by these malevolent spirits and display mild to severe bruises and bite marks, many of them in places where they could not be self-inflicted. Some researchers have noted that women occasionally have torn vaginal tissue after an alleged attack by an incubus. And how can science explain the many cases of spirit attack that are witnessed by others or happen to two people simultaneously? Clearly, science has not entirely explained these phenomena.

My advice to you, should you experience an attack by an evil spirit, is first to consult your doctor and ask about treatment for the common complaint of sleep paralysis. If you remain unconvinced as to that cause and feel that a malevolent spirit has indeed been making its presence known, you must not give in to fear. As with the thought-forms I spoke of earlier, these things feed upon our own energy, particularly the powerful energy of fear. If we persistently refuse to feed it with energy, we deprive it of the life force that energizes it.

Unfortunately, the peace and comfort provided by a belief in traditional religion may be compromised by religious fanatics who use the fear of demons to terrorize their flocks and encourage financial contributions to their cause. Under the cloak of religious teachings, some hold incendiary torches ready, with nothing to stop them except the critical reasoning of thinking individuals. Casting out demons, for example, to bring about on-call "miracles" makes exciting church, but whether the healing effect is real or the message is in any way true to the teachings of Jesus is debatable. Most enigmatic "healing" can be explained by autosuggestion, and the psychological manipulation of vulnerable people. I may be mistaken, but I prefer to believe that the humble carpenter's teachings are about love and tolerance rather than devils and demons. In whatever religious guise, the love of God is a powerful means of protection from all forms of negativity, so long as it comes from the heart and is not polluted by those with their agenda for fame and power.

On a more down to earth note, several folk remedies are said to protect sleepers from night attacks. A peony flower taken to bed or a cauldron in the room is specific to keeping away the incubus, while bluebells or phallic-shaped magical tools are supposed to ward off the succubus. These things reinforce your feeling of being safe.

Simple rituals can help some people strengthen the aura and protect against harm in daily life or as they sleep. You may, for example, wear a crystal or talisman to strengthen your faith in your protective energy. This could be a religious symbol, such as the Star of David or a cross, or something personal that will help you achieve a positive state of mind--perhaps a locket with a photo of a loved one.

Similarly, burning essential oils or placing a bowl of water in the sleeping room helps create a protected atmosphere. Hanging specific pictures in this area may inspire positive thoughts at bedtime. By creating a safe place to sleep or work and perhaps following a short ritual in a special place, you can help improve your own and the environment's positive energy. A ritual need only take a few minutes and is helpful to focus your attention and intent.

Many of the fears associated with paranormal events are a reflection of psychological processes. A tempting hypothesis is that many supernatural occurrences manifest the "dark side" of the human mind. The psychologist Carl G. Jung spoke about the part of ourselves that we reject and push away from our consciousness. For example, we may have childhood fears or current fears about our sexuality or death that we refuse to think about. We may also shun those things about ourselves that we would rather not know about-- our weaknesses, anxieties, and insecurities. These things are repressed, pushed into the unconscious part of our minds, to reappear suddenly in frightening dreams or irrational behaviour.

Jung called this frightening aspect of ourselves the Shadow. It is everything in us that is unconscious, repressed, undeveloped, and denied. However, to have a shadow even in the dark rejected aspects of our being, so there must be light; positive undeveloped potential that we don't recognize and don't know is there because it is in the unconscious. We all have such a shadow, and a confrontation with it is necessary to attain spiritual wholeness. Often we see this shadow side of our personality in other people. We may blame another for our faults and make them the scapegoats for our failings. Victims of their own irrational shadow do not take personal responsibility for their lives. Their failings are blamed on bad luck, bad omens, other people. Projection is an unconscious psychological mechanism. We all project onto other people aspects of ourselves that we deny and disown, and we refuse to identify with the projected quality or characteristic. It's them, not me!

Supposed evil influences are often projections of our hidden fears. The African slaves who were transported to Haiti, for example, brought with them their tribal superstitions and magical practices. These evolved and changed in line with the new conditions they faced. Coming from cultures that believed the universe to be a magical place, where man is born of magic, and all men are potential magicians, they naturally turned to sorcery to protect them from the hardships and injustices of slavery. One great fear was zombification. Zombies are people who appear dead and are buried but are later dug up and brought back to life. The sorcery was probably a trick, using a drug to put the unfortunate victim into a temporary coma. Haitians were so terrified of loved ones becoming zombies that corpses would be shot or strangled to save them from "lives" of enslavement. Zombie mythology is a reflection of the consciousness of enslaved people. During the struggle for independence, Haitian slaves vowed they would rather die than return to slavery. The zombie is a projection of the shadow of the slaves and represents their deepest fears. The zombie myth also fascinates people today, representing as it does our shadows and the aspects of our selves that we have buried.

Similarly, ghosts, haunting, magic, and superstition are often projections of our shadowy fears and, in particular, our worries about death and dying. This is why horror movies have such a popular appeal. They address the issues that frighten us and put a face to the monsters that we fear.

We conquer the fear of the shadow side of our selves when we gain spiritual illumination and self-knowledge, but few people understand the meaning of that term. "Self-knowledge" is widely confused with knowledge of one's day-to-day personality. True self-knowledge requires us to discover the unconscious side of ourselves. Here in the darkness lies our undiscovered self, and it is only by plunging into that shadow side of ourselves that we can discover our true nature. That's how we learn to face and to fight our inner demons. The result is that we no longer fear the unconscious or project these hidden fears into the world around us in the guise of malevolent spirits.

It may be that parts of ourselves that we reject may appear to us as something that can threaten or possess us. For example, Mother Teresa was clearly a holy person, yet letters written to her confessor reveal that she had many crises of faith. While so many looked to her for light and guidance, she was plagued with thoughts challenging to accept. "I am told God lives in me--and yet the reality of darkness and coldness and emptiness is so great that nothing touches my soul," she wrote in one letter. She too had her "dark night of the soul."

Perhaps she was trying to rid herself of these inner fears, hidden in the shadow side of herself when she had an exorcism performed on her in the later years of her life. This took place in a hospital in Kolkata, India, formerly known as Calcutta. The ritual of Catholic exorcism has its roots in the Bible, where it is described, in the New Testament, that Jesus healed afflicted people by casting out demons. Belief in the devil is one tenet of the church, and it teaches that Jesus gave his apostles and the church the power to rid people of evil spirits in his name.

The exorcism rite begins with the sign of the cross and the sprinkling of blessed water. The priest then reads a litany of the saints and seeks God's mercy. This is usually followed by a recitation of the Psalms, either by the priest or others' participation. Psalm-like prayers are usually said, and the Gospel read aloud as the priest lays his hands upon the afflicted person while invoking the Holy Spirit. The Catholic Creed is recited, baptismal promises are renewed, Satan is denounced, and then the Lord's Prayer is recited. The priest displays the cross and traces the sign of the cross on the possessed person's forehead. He then uses an imperative formula that begins with "I order you, Satan ..." and goes on to denounce Satan as "prince of the world" and "enemy of salvation." It ends with, "Therefore, go back, Satan." The rite concludes with a song or chant of thanksgiving, another prayer and a blessing.

I am confident that Mother Teresa had no real demons. It was her shadow self that she feared. Charity's Missionaries are feeding 500,000 families, treating 90,000 leprosy patients and educating 2,000 children each year in Kolkata alone. Her work on behalf of the poor won her the Nobel Peace Prize in 1979. She has lived according to the true love that was taught by Jesus and should have no fear of retribution from demons. But even the saintly push their fears into the darkness of the unconscious, where they can grow and fester until they are mistaken as something demonic.

Black Magic Thought Form

"Do what thou wilt shall be the whole of the law."
--**Aleister Crowley** (occultist)

Most people have inner fears that occasionally manifest in some irrational way. Thoughts that people find unacceptable are relegated to the fringes of consciousness. Denied and repressed, these thoughts tend to result in illogical behaviour or compulsive fears. This is often the case when people believe spirits are attacking that. Afraid "of their own shadow," instead of accepting that the problem is within, they look beyond the physical even to the spiritual world for an explanation of their fears. This aspect of psychology may explain many reports of demonic attack and evil spirits. However, the mind's power can also influence the world around us, and these repressed energies can take on physical form to impact the world by psychokinesis.

I spoke earlier of "mind fields" and how they surround individuals, places, and groups of people. I have cited a case from Tibetan mysticism in which a Tulpa entity is created from the meditating monk's mind and how this entity took on a life of its own. Similar reports from other cultures about spirits were born of the mind, which became temporary independent beings. They likely have no self-sustaining consciousness or sense of self but act out their creator's original motivations. I have myself investigated many so-called haunted houses and reports of spirit attack, and I believe that many of these are not spirits at all but thought forms that have taken on an energy of their own. Once brought into being, they continue to feed on the energy and the fear of those people who come in contact with them. Like the Tulpas of Tibet or the Genies of Arabia, these thought forms have no self-awareness; they react to us but have no will of their own.

One powerful example of a deliberately created mind form happened to a close friend of mine, a very powerful medium. My friend is a very level-headed woman, not someone prone to fantasy or exaggeration. At the time, her group was working with a distressed young man who had become involved in a Black Coven. He now wanted to break free because of the unsavoury sexual activities that some members were practising. The coven must have found out about what was happening and, as her group sat in meditation for their trance séance, all Hell broke loose.

"As soon as we sat, I was 'controlled' by something which filled my mind with abominations," she says. "I saw an altar draped in black cloth with black candles placed upon it, and I was being dragged towards it. I screamed, and then vile and vicious language and abuse spilt forth from my mouth. I was utterly unable to stop what was happening.

"The control left me, and I was myself again, hugely relieved. Then, within two minutes, I was cackling like some demonic hag threatening myself. This went on for a while, changing from me to a monster and back again and being unable to stop the changing from taking place.

"By this time, I was on the point of total hysteria. Our healer friend came across saying 'that's enough!' and gave me healing which cleared whatever was attached to me or using me."

For my medium friend, a thoughtful and very stable person, to have come out with "vile and vicious language" is entirely out of character. As a leading mediumistic teaching organization tutor, she explains to her students that there is nothing to fear in developing mediumship, for spirits cannot harm us if we work within the right conditions. "I believe that, in this instance, the Coven had sat down and created, with mind power, a thought form and directed it toward us," she says. "It attached itself to me when I was most vulnerable. If I had known that thought forms could be so powerful, perhaps I could have protected myself from what happened. I was shaken by what happened but not, I believe, harmed in any way. My problem was the same problem that infects all new mediums, thinking I could take on the world on my own and walk where 'angels fear to tread'."

Fortunately, at that sitting, a mutual friend of ours was present and could break the connection with the Coven's thought-form. This incident happened to my friend at the early stages of her trance work. Future mediumistic meetings had no further problems. Rarely is a person vulnerable, in a mediumistic circle, for we are protected by the group's collective energy, which shines around us like a brilliant light. In the instance cited above, the group was unaware that such a thought-form had been projected towards them, and they proceeded without adequate preparation. Recognizing that you are dealing with a thought-form helps you disperse its energy. Spiritual healing can help do this, too, breaking the attachment that a thought form has to an individual. The knowledge that it is "not real" also helps dissipate the fear associated with these things. Similarly, cheerfulness and laughter are potent weapons.

Earthbound Spirits

"There is a condition worse than blindness, and that is seeing something that isn't   there."
--**Ron Hubbard** (founder of Scientology)

Earthbound spirits is the term given to souls that have not been able to progress to the afterlife. They are the central theme of Hollywood's ghosts and spooks, and a great deal of misunderstanding has arisen about these things. Just about all of the many cases on which I have been asked to help are either the result of overactive imaginations or other manifestations of psychic power. For example, objects that move by themselves or fly about are often caused by a living person with an emotional problem. Their spiritual energy is under such tension that it cannot find a release in everyday life; it, therefore, explodes as a physical manifestation. (Sometimes, the earth energy of certain places can amplify this paranormal phenomenon.)

Repressed anger or sexual fears may result in the psyche's energy escaping in such a way that it can move objects or manifest as poltergeist activity. These people generate powerful thought forms that can influence the world around them or appear as ghostly phenomena. There are many instances on record of phantoms of living people. These often occur in times of crisis. For example, one woman wrote to me, saying, "We emigrated to Ontario, Canada, where my father worked in the steel plant. Dad was very ill and sick in bed when I went with my friends to the club. On the way home, I said, "Here comes Dad to meet us." There was no mistaking him, and we all saw him, a miner, short, bandy-legged with his flat cap on his head. I rushed towards him, wondering how he had recovered so quickly, but as I approached, he was gone." In this instance, the father was still alive when the group saw him.

Many phantom encounters involve some life crisis, most frequently the crisis of death. In the example I quoted above, the ill man died soon after the girls saw the vision. Apparitions of the living may manifest themselves for no particular reason. Many people have written to me of seeing their doubles or of being separated from the body and performing mundane tasks. The person projecting the phantom is entirely oblivious to what is happening, yet observers see the phenomena.

Similarly, groups of people who have no emotional connection to the deceased are experienced ghosts and hauntings. Hospitals, museums, mansions, and houses of all sorts, dilapidated or not, have been the abodes of human or animal ghosts. And, as well as individual ghosts, witnesses report seeing ghost trains, ships, long-sunken submarines or phantom armies fighting ancient battles.

One interesting example from my own experiences was a woman who claimed that a spirit was sexually molesting her. My initial reaction was that this was either someone with a severe psychological complaint or perhaps suffering from sleep paralysis. However, Spiritualists who contacted me regarding her claim reported witnessing a lot of poltergeist activity related to the "attacks."

When the woman showed me around her modern apartment and explained the places where the phenomena happened, I felt no particular negativity. However, I could undoubtedly feel negative vibrations connected to the woman herself. I believed the phenomena was coming from her, as projected energy, but how could I prove this to her? My solution was to sit with her and connect to someone she knew in spirit. Using my mediumistic ability, I gave her rock-solid evidence of her dead father. Once she was absolutely sure that I was indeed in contact with him, I then asked him to tell us what was the source of the poltergeist activity. He confirmed that it was his daughter's own energy and that she needed some counselling and healing to get her back into balance.

It is not easy to tell someone that they have not seen a ghost; that the phenomenon troubling them emanates from them. However, it is often the living that creates this frightening vicious circle of poltergeist activity fueled by fear. To stop the manifestation, victims must understand that they are the source of the phenomena. To protect themselves from these things, they simply have to stop being afraid.

Psychic Attachment

I have explained that many ghosts are psychic imprints that have been left behind, rather like a photograph, and that our own mental energy can sometimes create them. However, there are rare instances where real spirits attach themselves to a place and may cause upset and discord. Mediums call these spirits "earthbound" because a strong attachment is holding them to this plane and preventing them from progressing to the afterlife. In some instances, the spiritual entity does not realize that he or she is dead; they walk around our world in a somnambulistic state.

The famous Spiritualist "exorcist" Carl Wickland claimed that sometimes these lost souls were attracted to the warmth of the human aura and, under certain circumstances, may attach themselves to its owner as a kind of mental parasite. From the spirits' standpoint, it may be completely unaware of what is happening or that it has connected with the living person. This is quite a rare condition and cannot occur if your aura and your soul are in harmony. It can, however, happen to people who are in an unstable mental state. In these cases, real phenomena may occur.

A striking example happened when a psychologist called to see if I could help her with one of her patients. The person was convinced that the only way she could stop hearing the voices was if she saw a medium. Eventually, the psychologist relented and asked me if I would accompany her to the woman's house. Naturally, having a trained scientific background, the psychologist was sceptical and believed that psychology could explain it. However, her tone changed when we entered the house and were surrounded by a strange mist that flowed around the floor. "D-d-did, you see that!" she stuttered, her face as white as the proverbial ghost. I did, and it was clear that we were dealing with real phenomena.

The woman in question was, I agreed afterwards, mentally unstable, but her fear was being stimulated by a spirit man that had attached itself to her. Also, the strange phenomena that we were witnessing were, of course, not helping matters! To sever this unwelcome bond, I sat in meditation and made contact with the offending spirit. The man I described was a burly gipsy who claimed that he was buried near the house. He had various emotional worries, but he also was unaware that he was dead. He thought he had been attending someone else's funeral! Eventually, I convinced him to move on and connect with the spirit people who were trying to help him pass over to the next stage of life. The atmosphere changed as the weight was lifted, and the strange clouds faded away.

Later, the psychologist rang me to say that the woman was feeling better and had been helped by what had happened. She now felt she could sleep in her own house again. She, too, had been shaken by what she witnessed, and more so after she had done a little research into the area. Although no gipsy graveyard was marked on the map, she had found references in the library to confirm that gipsies were said to have buried or cremated their dead in that area.

Again, fear is at the root of these problems. In this case, the earthbound spirit's fear was transferred to the aura of the living person. In turn, the living person's fear upset the spirit, creating a cycle of fear. Although a medium may encourage a trapped spirit to move forward to the next world, there is a lot that can be done without such assistance. It is essential that the person under attack regain emotional and mental equilibrium. The person involved may be mentally healthy but have emotional problems that make them susceptible. These issues need to be addressed before the release can take place.

If the person has severe emotional difficulties or exhibits strange behaviour, seek professional help from a psychiatrist or counsellor. A person suffering from the onset of schizophrenia would be much better helped by somebody trained in this field than by a well-meaning medium or psychic. Schizophrenia is a clinical condition that can be treated if caught in its early stages. Leave this one to the experts.

Ghost Busting

"Who you gonna call."
--from the film *Ghostbusters*

The first thing to do if someone reports that they are experiencing poltergeist activity is, of course, to ascertain whether there is a normal explanation for what has been happening. Perhaps the "poltergeist" is a noisy pipe, a draft, a prankster, and/or the result of an overactive imagination. It is worth noting that researchers have noticed that real poltergeist activity usually manifests in many different ways. You get repetition, not exactly the same thing, but similarities between events. If the poltergeist activity always follows the same pattern, and the person reporting them appears to have all the answers, I would advise you to be suspicious of the reports. However, if the person is completely perplexed by what has been happening and does not appear to be an attention seeker, the reported instance may be worthy of investigation.

In every genuine poltergeist case, I have encountered there has been a background factor of high emotional stress. I am convinced that poltergeist activity is somehow caused by this emotional stress, either in the form of projected psychological energy alone or with the influence of spirits that have connected to this mind field. Sometimes I feel a bit sorry for the spirit who has become entangled in the "victim's" mind field. No wonder they sometimes become angry, frustratingly trapped in a web of fear and intense emotional energy! Nonetheless, in either instance, the priority is to remove the cause of the problem, the high stress that fuels these events.

To deal with the situation, it is important to win the people's confidence involved by listening to them. This may reveal the anxieties causing the energy that fuel the phenomena. Naturally, it's hoped that the medium will take care of everything for them; but those afflicted need to understand that it can be done only with their co-operation. Although some spirits may be involved, the key to solving the problem is to help the witnesses find the right frame of mind to establish a degree of natural psychic protection. They must come to understand that they are part of the process of restoring harmony.

After removing a troublesome sprit from a location, I have at times left feeling unsatisfied because the person at the centre of the activity has not resolved his or her inner stress or been willing to address the issue. It is, therefore, possible that, like a magnet, they will attract or create new phenomena. Right from the start, it is best to tell a person, "We can sort this out together," instead of something on the order of, "I can get rid of this thing." Again, this will involve a lot of listening.

The only way to get rid of the problem is to reduce stress. A priest doing an exorcism may achieve this end, but it may also inadvertently cause added fear and further fuel the stress. Similarly, "mediums" prone to fantasy may make all sorts of unsubstantiated claims about the spirits involved. This can only make matters worse for the already frightened witnesses. No, grandiose claims of "I can deal with it" do not get to the heart of the matter. It is up to us to empower the witnesses to know that they can deal with it themselves.

I like to sit and meditate in the place that is the epicenter of the trouble with my own work. I will open my mind to the spirit influences and, once contact has been made (and verified), I encourage the spirit to progress to the higher life. Usually, this is not that hard to achieve, for there is already a natural pull being extended from the next life to encourage the spirit person to let go. They, too, may have a lot of fear about doing just that, and it has been exaggerated further by the witnesses' mind-field. I may suggest that they think of someone they love who has gone on, so that spirit will draw near and now help them cross over.

If the witnesses are involved in this communication, it can, if done properly with an easygoing attitude and in good humor, remove the influence and, most importantly, reduce the people's stress. Maintaining this new attitude is, of course, a lot more complicated. Suppose the witnesses are very superstitious or believe that they are being attacked by black magic, voodoo, and so on. In that case, it is going to take further counselling to reduce the stress to a level where all activity stops. Nonetheless, stress reduction is, I believe, the key to solving this type of problem. To help maintain the improved state of mind, a charm amulet or simple ritual can be used to reassure and help amplify this sense of protection. We will now consider some techniques involving protection from negative spirits and from negative energy in general.

Protective Rituals and Techniques

"Rituals are superstitions; they are adventitiously reinforced. The more conspicuous and stereotyped the behaviour upon which the reinforcer is accidentally contingent, the greater the effect."
-- Skinner, B. F. (behavioural scientist)

A protective atmosphere is established by creating the right mental attitude. Some people can do this naturally or have learned to do it through mediumistic training, self-observation, NLP, observances, yoga, meditation, and so on. Others use a focal point to help them attain this protective inner state, and some may benefit from ritual, ceremony, and invocation. Religion, magic, and folklore all use such techniques to bring the practitioner into transcendent states of consciousness.

Since the dawn of humanity, rituals have been with us when early man painted their dead in ochre to symbolize new blood and the promise of rebirth. Some of these may seem very strange to us today. For example, in medieval times, burglars believed that they would become invisible if they carried a lighted candle made from dead babies' fat. According to Roman historians, the British Celts made giant wicker "men" in which prisoners were placed and burned alive as sacrifices to call down the fertility gods' protection. In many parts of the world today, it is customary to dance around the "Maypole" to bring fertility to the women and cattle.

We see echoes of ancient rituals in our modern lives, too. Take Christmas, for example. Strange practices persist, yet we are oblivious to their meaning. Did you know that kissing under the mistletoe is a remnant of old Druid fertility rites, or that the Christmas tree, with its angel perched on top, is a carryover from when fairylike tree spirits were worshipped? A pine tree was once sacred to the deity Attis and the Great Mother of Gods, Cybele, in a cult brought to Rome from Phrygia in 204 B.C. To celebrate, devotees hung gold and silver ornaments upon the tree, placed the image of a sacred bird in its branches, and left sacrificial gifts underneath. Evergreens were considered symbols of rebirth and used as protective charms against the machinations of evil forces. The Yuletide Tree was sacred to the Teutonic god Woden as a symbol of eternal life. Similarly, the pagans believed that holly had extraordinary protective powers, a large bunch was traditionally hung in doorways.

Nonetheless, if we can clear the ritual of its superstition, we have something useful. Ritual can help us to create appropriate states of mind to use mental energy to influence the world around us and to protect us from negative influences. As this book is primarily about protecting the soul, I will now suggest some simple ways to use ritual to create protective mental energy.

Charms

When I was a child, I remember being fascinated by the rabbit's foot that my grandfather kept on his key ring. He had told me it was to bring good luck and keep evil away. The foot of a rabbit is a good luck charm around the world. It had its origin because young rabbits are born with their eyes open, thus able to "see off" evil from the moment they come into the world. Some mothers believe that brushing their newborn baby with a rabbit's foot will protect it from lifelong harm. Poachers think that if they carry a rabbit's foot in their pocket, they will never be caught.

Many strange superstitions persist in our society, and they come from many different traditions. One of my favourite, from Germany, advises us to wear our pockets inside out to ward off evil. Germans also say that if you are bewitched, you should boil a beef heart and, while it is cooking, keep sticking it with a needle. The witch will have the same pains, and the spell upon you will be broken. Another useful German remedy says that if you put a pair of scissors under your pillow, open with the points towards the head of the bed, no one can harm you or bewitch you. It works, but you may lose an ear in the process! (A recent survey found that Germany is the most superstitious European country, with one in three Germans believing in luck and charms. Britain and America follow close behind.)

One of the most well-known protective charms is the horseshoe, which brings good luck not only because it is shaped like a C to represent Christ and its curved shape symbolizes the heavens. The shoe is seen as being forged in the sacred fires and made from the sacred metal iron. No doubt, it fascinated early man, witnessing a shoe nailed on to protect a horse's foot, yet the animal felt no pain. These good luck charms are said to ward off evil and attract good fortune. The most common ones, and often found on charm bracelets, including crossed fingers, a cloverleaf, a shoe, the crescent moon, dice, a dog, wheel, toadstool, and the three monkeys: hear no evil, see no evil, and speak no evil. The most popular lucky charm of all is the figure of St. Christopher.

Some of America's most interesting superstitions come from the Irish. For example, St. Patrick is the patron saint of Ireland and is said to have driven the "snakes," i.e. the devil, from Ireland. We have adopted the shamrock (and in its rare form, the four-leaf clover) as a symbol of the "luck of the Irish," as clover grows plentiful in the green hills of Ireland. This Irish protective and lucky symbolism is now celebrated once a year on St. Patrick's Day and persists in the form of a famous cereal that includes moons, stars, hearts and clovers.

During the early 20th century, when many Irish Catholic men became police officers in New York City. Some believed that carrying a charm of St. Jude, along with their call box key, brought protection while on duty, as St. Jude is considered to be the patron saint of policemen. Similarly, some ballplayers swear by a pair of "lucky socks" to protect them from failure and hesitate to wash them during an important series for fear that they will lose power.

As an addition to European traditions, American culture has many influences from Africa. Returning to the topic of the rabbit foot, in ancient African culture, the carrying of an animal's foot, or other parts of a swift creature, was supposed to help a person escape or flee with the speed of the animal. Silver was prized as protection. Did you know that keeping a silver dime in your mouth will prevent you from being poisoned? Or that you can't be hoodooed if you wear a silver dime, particularly if it is worn around each ankle? A dime wrapped in brown paper and worn in the heel of your shoe protects from evil, but it also tends to give you blisters and cause you to limp in circles. A better protective remedy is to sprinkle grave dust, as this keeps witches away; if grave dust is not readily available, keep red pepper in your shoe at all times.

Research has shown women to be more superstitious than men. Psychologists believe that this is because women generally feel they have less control over their lives, so they have a greater need for protection. Being superstitious means believing that outside forces have power over you. Men are more likely to believe they are in charge of their own lives.

Not surprisingly, people get more superstitious when problems come up. That's why people whose jobs are insecure, like actors, are famously superstitious and can go to great lengths in the use of protective charms. The singer Barry Manilow, for example, insists that no one cross his path from the moment he enters his dressing room to the time he steps on stage. He even has a clause in his contract, stipulating this to make sure everyone respects it. Mick Jagger's ex-wife Jerry Hall always carries charms and touches wood, and Sophia Loren believes that luck will never desert her as long as she wears something red, even if no one can see it.

Of course, such foolish superstitions are only for other people. You wouldn't do anything like that, would you? Except, of course, when you get married. At that time, it seems, we go to some bizarre extremes to protect ourselves from bad luck.

Give a thought to the brides of the Galla tribe in Ethiopia. For good luck, fertility, and to ward off evil, the bride must, on her wedding day, stiffen her hair with butter and rub her body with civet, which makes it smell like cat urine! The wedding ceremony begins when the bridegroom climbs into the bride's lap and sits there while a mixture of butter and honey is poured over them. Consider, too, the men of the Macusi Indians in Guiana. To be virile--or perhaps henpecked?--enough for marriage, they must be sewn up in a hammock full of fire ants.

European superstitions are not quite messy or painful, but they have some peculiar nuptial superstitions of their own. Here are some left over from rituals of long ago.

It is unlucky for two sisters to marry two brothers. As there is only so much luck to go round, says superstition lore, someone's bound to lose out. It is also unlucky for a man to marry someone from his locality. This belief can be traced back to tribal days when a man would steal his bride from another tribe. The tradition continues by the carrying of the bride over the groom's threshold.

The phrase "tying the knot" dates back to very ancient times when the Babylonians would take a thread from the bride and groom's clothing and then symbolically tie the couple together. Timing of a marriage is important: Although it is unlucky to be married on your birthday, it is fortunate if you and your partner share the same birth date, although you must be a year or two apart. The luckiest month to tie the knot is June, named after Juno, the goddess of youth. She was the much loved and faithful wife of the Roman god Jupiter, who was revered as the protector of women. (Another reason for June weddings; in earlier times, marriage ceremonies took place at the church doors, and it was less likely to rain in June.) However, do not think of marrying in May for this woeful month was named after the Roman god Maia, the wife of Vulcan and patroness of the aged. She was definitely not a suitable deity to watch over young lovers.

Many of our superstitions about love and marriage originate from ancient times. For example, the wedding ring not only represents a magic circle of union between two people but is supposed to protect the bride against evil spirits. The tradition of placing a ring on the third finger comes from the mistaken ancient Greek belief that a vein runs from this finger directly to the heart. The wedding cake also featured in the wedding ceremony since ancient times, symbolizes fertility and good luck. It is lucky for the bride and groom to cut a cake together, as it represents their plan to live together. The Romans used to crumble a slice of cake over newlyweds to ensure their prosperity, but the ancient Chinese started the custom of giving a slice of cake to wedding guests and those who could not attend. Single girls would sleep with a piece of wedding cake under their pillows to dream of their future husbands. Many still do.

Every bride is still encouraged to wear "something old, something new; something borrowed and something blue." Superstition says that the "something old" should be her shoes or handkerchief and the "blue" part of her bouquet (a symbol of fertility). The white dress symbolizes innocence and purity to everyone except the Chinese bride. In that culture, white is the colour of mourning and is worn at funerals. To the Chinese, red is the lucky colour, so many of their marriage certificates are printed on red paper. For Europeans, the wearing of red to a wedding is an ill omen, but green is to be avoided at all costs; it is the fairies' colour, and they are liable to come and steal away anyone found wearing it.

It was legal in England until the thirteenth century to carry out "marriage by capture," a tradition that survives today as the bridegroom leading his best man and ushers to the ceremony. Likewise, the bridesmaids represent the "guards" entrusted to protect the bride from enemies wanting to carry her off. We can get some helpful tips about capture from the Banyankole tribe of Uganda. Here the groom holds down his bride while *her* family ties her up with ropes. As she weeps, the bride and groom's families have a tug of war. The groom's side is always allowed to win. As the groom whisks his bride away, the bride's family weeps and wails, calling for her to return. The more convincing the acting, the more successful the wedding.

The truth is that, although we may say that we are not superstitious, many of our familiar social rituals are full of magical symbolism designed to protect the soul. On a more serious note, it could be argued that when we cease to believe in superstitions, they are no longer effective, for they fail to awaken our protective spiritual energies. Nonetheless, a belief in a protective charm may have real benefits if it helps us to establish a confident mental attitude and--as I have argued earlier--creates a "mind field" of positive energy around us. For me, the most potent charms are those that remind me of God; for then, I am linked to the highest protective energy of all. And these charms need not necessarily be symbols. The only charms I carry are images of those who have attained God-consciousness-- such as the Christ, the Buddha, or a guru with whom I feel an affinity.

Talismans, Amulets and Spells

"Heaven is a field into which the imagination of man throws the seeds."
--Paracelsus (1493-1541),

The most powerful of charms are talismans. A talisman is any physical object that stores and radiates magical energy to create change or provide protection. Sometimes worn as a pendant, they often contain magical symbols or number sequences. The use of talismans appears to date back to early man.

Talismans are objects that embody an innate magical power that is transmitted to the possessor. Talismans are frequently confused with amulets, which passively protect the owner from evil and harm. Usually, a talisman's singular function is to make powerful transformations possible, but both amulet and talisman are used as protection. In ancient Egypt, the frog protected fertility, the Udjat Eye brought good health, and the scarab beetle symbolized resurrection. Two of the most famous amulets of ancient Egypt are the Eye of Horus and the Ankh. These symbols were believed to protect the wearer from evil.

The Arabs also had their protective amulets and, in particular, wore small sacks containing dust from tombs to protect them from evil. Similarly, the Hebrews wore crescent moons to ward off the evil eye and attached bells to their garments to ward off evil spirits.

Two of the most common cross-cultural symbols of amulets are the eye and phallic symbols. As eyes are thought to protect against evil spirits, they are found on tombs, walls, utensils, and jewellery.

Since ancient times, the phallic symbol, represented by horns and hands, has stood for protection against the evil eye. Similarly, the names of God and magical words and numbers have generally been thought to provide protection, so they have been made into amulets. Books of magical instruction called grimoires accompanied renaissance versions. Grimoires offered instructions on the making of talismans. Talismans were often inscribed on precious stones or parchment under auspicious astrological signs. They were used for getting rich, winning at gambling, falling in love, safeguarding against sudden death, improving memory, and even making a good speech.

Certain shapes have protective power. For example, the pentagram has been a protective sign against evil powers in the West and in Japan. In Nordic countries, it is found drawn on the doors of barns and storehouses to ward off trolls and invoke protecting powers. Similarly, the Star of David (also known as the shield of David) is an ancient protective symbol that is believed to date as far back as 800-600 B.C. The shape occurs today on Icelandic police badges and is echoed in the star found on the badges of some U.S. sheriffs.

One of the most powerful amulets to be worn as a pendant is the Sator-Rotas Square. It was discovered scratched on a wall in the buried city of Pompeii and dates back to the first century AD. Because of the hidden anagram, Pater Noster, the square was initially thought to be of Christian design, but there is strong evidence that it predates Christianity and refers to the ancient God, Mithras. This Persian God is usually depicted with a lion's head and wings. Mithras was the defender of light and truth and protector from evil. The Sator-Rotas Square is supposed to protect against sorcery, poisonous air, colic, and pestilence; and keep cow's milk safe from witchcraft. It was believed that the square had magical properties and that making it visible would ward off evil spirits. They are available today from many New Age shops and websites.

It is claimed that the Viking runes also bring protective power. A technique is to draw the runes onto the body with blood or, in the case of a fertility charm, to carve the runes on a piece of cheese and then eat it. For personal protection, one of the most used is the symbol *ægishjálmr* which, literally translated, means "helm of awe" or "helm of terror." One of these "helms" is claimed to imbue the owner with the power to strike paralyzing fear into the heart of an enemy. This runic symbol can be a powerful form of personal protection, and it is sometimes worn as a tattoo.

Many pagans wore figurines of their gods as amulets; similarly, bits of paper containing quotes from holy books are carried in pouches or worn in jewellery. The remnant of this custom continues in the Catholic religion, where some members still wear scapulars and medals of the saints. For example, Catherine de Medici, queen consort of Henry II of France, wore a medal made from metals melted together during favourable astrological signs and mixed with human and goat's blood. Although the original was broken at her death, a copy exists in the Bibliotheque Nationale in Paris. On one side of the medal is engraved the god Jupiter, the eagle of Ganymede, and a demon with the Egyptian god Anubis's head. On the reverse is a Venus figure, believed to be Catherine, flanked by demons. She believed the talisman protected her and gave her clairvoyance and sovereign power

Spells

There was a time when just about everyone believed in the power of magic, and particularly in the power of spells. We need not look far back in our history to read of how the spells and hexes of witches were held responsible for many of the troubles of society. A witch would cast her spells under the moon on a Friday night and meet with the devil in a meadow or graveyard. If witchcraft was thought to be the cause of a problem, there were many counter-charms a person could use, such as carrying salt, bread, or spitting over the left shoulder.

During the Middle Ages, the churches denounced witches, and there followed two hundred years of "witch hunts." The most famous American case took place in Salem, Massachusetts, in 1692, when a West Indian slave named Tituba scared young girls into fits with her terrifying voodoo stories. The doctors of the town decided that the girls had been bewitched. To protect herself, Tituba began to accuse others of casting spells. This, in turn, led to other hysterical accusations, resulting in twenty-two people being put to death for casting spells.

It is no wonder that the casting of spells went out of fashion. Today, protection against witchcraft continues in our superstitions.

For example, some buildings in the Dutch section of Pennsylvania have been painted in the protective colour red and bear "hex signs" to frighten away evil spirits and counterspells against the householders. The old beliefs persist, but there has also been a renaissance in magic in recent years. Instead of instilling fear, the modern practitioner of Wicca, or paganism, turns to the old religions as an ancient system of influencing the world for the better. They claim that in the days before the church's influence, witchcraft's actual practice lay not in the Christian's devil but in using the power of love to influence the world.

Today, many people turn to spells and spell makers to help them achieve their goals. There is an interest in spells to help us fall in love and stay in love. Again, candle burning helps cast these spells, but candle-burning also helps the practitioner focus and relax. Spells are often spoken under the moonlight, as this symbolises the illumination of the inner world and the love that spreads from inside us. The moon is also believed to open the door to intuition and help you learn the secrets of your loved one's heart. The spells and paraphernalia of Wicca are meaningless in themselves. The most important thing about spells is not their complexity or origin but that they hold a special meaning to you. For a spell to work, there has to be belief.

A spell of protection can be taken from tradition, or you can make one up yourself. When casting a spell, it is important to establish the right setting. You may want to use various devices such as candles, gemstones, oils, or some other paraphernalia. Most important, however, are the right intentions and the right state of mind. And, of course, you need to accept that they can work. If all this is in place, then spells can be a powerful way to increase personal protection. They are essentially an inner mental affirmation that can generate its own protective energy.

Tradition says that spells are best performed following the lunar cycle. Spells of "increase," such as gaining a new job, attracting a lover or increasing personal power, are done on a waxing moon. Spells of "decrease," such as to end a financial difficulty or string of bad luck or to remove a negative influence, are best done during the waning moon. It is said that spells get better with practice and become more effective as you put more of yourself into them.

Sometimes protective spells are accompanied by rituals, such as placing crossed needles under the doormat, burning sage, or washing all the windows with vinegar! Spells can also be written on paper, burned, and the ashes carried in a spell bottle.

Mantras

"Chant the Gayatri as often as possible. If you chant it while you take a bath, your bath gets sanctified. Likewise, chant it before taking your food. The food becomes an offering to the divine. Develop heartfelt devotion to God."
--Sathya Sai Baba

Mystical traditions believe that certain words have the power to transform our soul and can act as a powerful protection from harm. When chanted, these are called a mantra. Mantra is a Sanskrit word with many meanings. Some consider it to be "divine speech." They are believed to increase spiritual awareness, heal, and can bring about favourable circumstances for those who chant them. They are ancient formulas recorded by the ancient sages of India.

The oldest mantras, and arguably the most powerful, come from India's holy scriptures called the Vedas. Nobody knows when they were first created. The teachings were transmitted by oral tradition and are believed to be over 5,000 years old. The historical writer Graham Hancock argues that they may date back 11,000 years and are relics from the civilizations that thrived just after the last Ice Age. Like an Eastern version of The Legend of Atlantis, the ruins of this lost civilization now lie under the ocean to the south of the Indus Valley, swallowed as the waters rose when the polar ice caps melted.

There are four Vedas: the Rig, Sama, Yajur, and Atharva. Each Veda itself is composed of parts, the Samhita (the mantras in verse), the Brahmana (rituals and liturgy in prose) and the Aranyakas and Upanishads (the philosophical works). Many believe that the Vedas are eternal scriptures, "heard" by ancient seers and collected by them. The Rigveda Samhita contains 1,028 suktas (hymns) with a total of 10,552 mantras (verses) arranged in ten books.

Considered by many to be the most ancient and holy of the mantras is the Gayatri mantra. Legend has it that the mantra was rediscovered by a rishi called Vishwamitra, a king who went through many arduous struggles to attain spiritual insight. The mantra, it is said, protects the individual and eventually transforms the whole of humanity by bringing enlightenment to all. This mantra is believed to bring great benefit. Its powerful words are charged to keep you to the light and drive away all negativity.

I was moved by it when I first heard it in India, echoing through the temples of the ashram I was visiting. Seated on the dusty ground, I could have been living thousands of years ago when the first avatars walked the earth. One of my friends, travelling with us, was a Sanskrit scholar and made sure that every word we chanted was precisely correct. The more perfect the pronunciation, we were told, the greater the benefit the mantra brings, for its sounds correspond directly with the higher vibrations of the spirit. I found it a little tricky at first, but even incorrect pronunciation brings some benefit. This mantra can be used anytime and, should you feel fearful for any reason, it will generate spiritual light and protection.

The Enlightenment Mantra

Om Bhur Bhuva Suvah
Tat Savithur Varenyam
Bhargo Devasya Dheemahi
Dhiyo Yonah Prachodayat

Pronunciation

OM BOO BOO-VAH-HAH SWAH-HA
TAHT SAH-VEE-TOOR VAHR-EHN-YUM
BHAHR-GO DEH-VAHS-YAH DEE-MAH-HEE
DEE-YOH YOHN-NAH PRAH-CHOH-DAH-YAHT

The meaning of the mantra: We meditate on that most adorable, most desirable and most enchanting lustre (effulgence) of our supreme Lord, who is our creator, inspirer and source of eternal Joy. May this light inspire and illumine our intellect (and dispel the darkness).

Breakdown of the meanings of individual words: **Aum:** The primaeval sound (from which all sounds emerge); **Dheemahi:** We meditate upon; **Varenyam:** the most adorable, most desirable or most enchanting; **Bhargo**: lustre or effulgence; **Tat**: of that; **Devasya**: supreme (Lord); **Savitur**: from whom all creations emerge (also means the Sun God who is our life source); **Bhur**: who is our inspirer; **Bhuvah**: who is our creator; **Suvaha**: who is the abode of supreme joy; (**Bhur**, **Bhuvah** and **Suvaha** are also considered to mean three lokas or worlds namely Heaven, earth and lower worlds). **Yo**: May this light; **Prachodayaat**: inspire/illumine; **Naha**: our; **Dhiyo**: intellect (activities of the intellect).

5 PROTECTING YOUR SOUL DAILY

"I've developed a new philosophy... I only dread one day at a time."
--Charlie Brown (artist Charles Schulz)

Have you ever met someone who drains you of energy? They may be well-meaning, but something about them leaves you weak and exhausted. One person I know, for example, often says, "What you need is a big hug!" However, if you are unfortunate enough to receive the offered "comfort," you are left feeling far worse than before! Such people can drain all your energy simply by shaking your hand or talking to you. And they are everywhere! We mediums call them "psychic vampires."

Psychic vampires are people who do their damage by a telepathic draining of their victim's auric energy, affixing themselves to it like a parasite. They are usually dominant, extrovert, and highly talkative. In extreme cases, they are very intense and sometimes slightly manic. In these individuals, fear is typically present in the background of their consciousness. It would be best if you learned to protect yourself from their negative influences.

If a psychic vampire becomes a close friend or a partner, the long-term effect can be very harmful. At first, neither of you will realize what is happening, but gradually you will become debilitated and lack motivation and energy. The victims of psychic draining usually have an emaciated physique, a pallid complexion, and an overall sense of weakness. They are often suggestible people and the complete opposite in many ways to those who display psychic vampirism.

Psychic vampirism is often present in people who have a degree of paranoia or repressed fear. This type of person may be stubborn and hold bigoted views. They like to win arguments. Never argue with this sort of person, as you will never win. They want an argument to prove to themselves that they are better than you are. It's best to simply back away from this type of person and even avoid eye contact. Speak to them in a soothing low voice and try to change the topic of conversation to something pleasant

The same draining can also happen when you meet overtly extrovert people. Often the "life and soul of the party" is someone who drains the life from the partygoers! People who like to be the centre of attention may seek to drain everyone's energy. We see celebrities who love their public's adoration; they often speak of how it gives them a "high" to have all this energy directed at them. The same can occur at political rallies, in theatres, public meetings, or even during a demonstration of mediumship in a Spiritualist Church. In these instances, the person who is the centre of attention can be uplifted but without detriment to others. In a one-to-one situation, however, an entertaining person can also be spiritually draining.

Insecurity can also cause a person to become a psychic vampire. Something may have happened to them in their past, giving them a fear of abandonment and anxiety that the problems will reoccur. They may think that everyone drains their energy, so their response is to compensate by taking the energy from others. These people may make you feel depressed or tired. They may engage in boring conversation and come across as helpless and dependent on others.

It is advisable not to be drawn into trying to solve this sort of person's perceived problems. They may enjoy thinking that they are the victim and may not necessarily be looking for a self-empowering solution to their behaviour problem. If their depression is clinical, they may need medical assistance. Sometimes these individuals live in constant fear of rejection and abandonment. You may give them some words of encouragement and optimism but do not necessarily try to solve their problems.

A great many people adopt negative mental habits that prevent them from being a self-sufficient individual. These habits can be subliminal, but they still result in their becoming emotionally dependent on others. This type of personality, again, is likely to drain the energy from your aura. They strive to involve other people in their lives and make demands on them. Living from moment to moment, they have no structure in their lives or plans for the future. This type of individual may be prone to fantasy, have a deep sense of isolation, and resent self-dependent people. This may result in a wave of muffled anger towards others which taints the energy they project. Helping this sort of person can be problematic. They will be very creative in their ability to find reasons to reject your advice.

Psychic vampires lurk in unexpected places and are sometimes successful people. People driven by the need for personal power may draw from the energy of the people around them. These people may have high-paying jobs, a good reputation, a perfect spouse and family, and look in perfect health, but they never really draw any real satisfaction from life. They often find it hard to engage intellectually or emotionally with other people and maintain a continual sense of urgency. Again, this type of person can quickly deplete your energy, and it is best to avoid them if possible. If you are drawn to this type of person, you may find that their power is increased at your expense.

It is best not to look these people in the eye. Not only are the eyes an important part of human communication, but yogis believe that energy is projected through them as well. Some people think the left eye is the passive one so, if circumstances dictate that you meet the gaze of a person displaying psychic vampirism, it is better to look only at the left eye. Similarly, folding the arms, crossing your ankles or legs, and placing your folded arms across your solar plexus are ways to protect vulnerable areas of the aura. It is also best not to sit or stand directly facing an energy vampire. I mentioned earlier about visualizing a mirror or a shield to deflect negative vibrations and gain protection from bad energy. Another simple technique--preferred by some--is to imagine the negative energy passing straight through your aura without affecting it at all.

Fear Energy in Everyday Life

Various forms of fear drive all the psychic vampires I have mentioned. From a spiritual perspective, fear is a vibration as well as a state of mind. Fear vibrations attack the aura like daggers or bolts of electricity. You feel uneasy if your aura field comes into contact with someone whose vibration generates these feelings of friction. Sometimes it is evident that the person harbours bad feelings towards you, but there are times when the negative signals are hidden. It is the "atmosphere" of a person that reveals their true intent. Prolonged exposure to hidden malicious feelings may make you feel tense and uncomfortable.

Before becoming self-employed, I shared an office with someone who was a persistent worrier. He was always imagining all sorts of troubles looming on the horizon. When problems did arise, he would perceive them to be far worse than they were. After a few months of being subjected to this negativity, I realized that I was beginning to mirror his behaviour. I was becoming a bag of nerves and erroneously believed that my life was lurching from crisis to crisis. This happened when I had some real difficulties, but being surrounded by a chronic worrier made matters much worse. Eventually, I changed my circumstances, and in a very short period, all of my troubles evaporated. I was back on track. I had learned that worry not only undermines your self-confidence and brings troubles to you, but that it can also be transmitted from one person to another.

Worry is a form of fear and is one form of negative energy that is likely to undermine you in your day-to-day contact with others. In the instance I just described, this person's fear is habitual. Many people are like this. They have established self-destructive behaviour patterns that are also destructive to the people around them. It is bad energy. It can also spread to a larger group of people. For example, when the Beatles first started performing, they planted a few screaming girls in the audience. Soon the mood spread until everyone was in a state of hysteria. Moods can influence the mind-fields of whole communities in this way.

Nature provided us with the emotion of fear for a reason. It is a warning that we are in danger and triggers bodily reactions to fight or flee the potential hazard. Adrenaline is released into the bloodstream, our heart pounds faster, our body feels more vigorous, and our senses become more acute. Rational fear brings awareness of danger and empowers a person. Fear can be pleasurable and exciting when the danger element is handled or controlled, such as when taking a ride on a roller coaster or parachuting.

Worry as a habitual fear may occur when people feel they are not in control of their circumstances. The worries may be out of proportion to the known facts because they refuse to accept a situation or feel that they are not strong enough to cope. This creates a cycle of quiet despair that may prevent them from functioning to their true potential. Often there are hidden anxieties that fuel this worry. Past failures and chastisement during childhood may result in patterns of behaviour that undermine a person's confidence. A great deal of habitual worry may stem from irrational forces that unconsciously motivate us.

When we encounter extreme negativity situations, it is good to join with others to cleanse these vibrations and share positive energy. Group meditation increases the energy of all the participants. It is an example of the whole being greater than the sum of its parts. Everyone's energy is increased without anyone being depleted in any way. In effect, we draw from the cosmic energy that is all around us. It is beneficial in times of world crisis for people to gather together and to focus on positive energy. The good energy we generate acts as a protection for the individual and may influence the future. Compassionate thoughts have wings. Flying into the darkness, they carry our healing love.

We encounter fear vibrations in many settings. Everywhere we go, "psychic vampires" are ready to drain our spiritual energy. They may be individuals or manifestations of collective influences that lie in wait to do us harm. For example, global vibrations during wartime, influences in troubled communities that are poorly policed, dealings as we go about our day-to-day activities--at home, school, work, and so on--may suck away at us. The truth is that we are sublimely affected by the world conditions and the worries and inner traumas of people we meet, and these things can pollute or drain our auric light. We need to find ways to safeguard ourselves.

Personal Protection

"Only the dead are without fear."
--Yul Brynner, *The Magnificent Seven*

Most of the time, we are protected from fear vibrations because the aura is closed to negative influences. It remains close to the body and is covered by an auric shield--something like the shell of an egg. This prevents most vibrations from affecting us. However, continual psychic attack from other people's bad vibrations at a subliminal level may weaken this protection. In addition, our guard drops when we feel tired or depressed or have been in an environment where the negative energy is intense. Sometimes a negative individual may strip us of our natural protection.

In these situations, it is vital to strengthen the aura. Doing this will help you to maintain inner tranquillity, and it has the added benefit of increasing your vitality and health. One method of doing this is by using special breathing techniques.

The ancient practice of yoga recognizes that breath is important for our well-being. It gives us the oxygen we need to stay alive, but according to the yogis, it draws the life force into the body. In India, they call this life force prana. Prana (also known as Chi in China and Ki in Japan) are sparks of finer-than-atomic energy, which the Indian guru Paramahansa Yogananda translated as "lifetrons." Prana takes two forms: the cosmic vibratory energy that is omnipresent in the universe, structuring and sustaining all things, and the specific aura that sustains each human body.

By consciously controlling our breathing (pranayama), we can draw prana energy into our aura and increase our life force. This will make us feel more alive and vital and thereby strengthen our aura. This will cleanse us and protect us from exposure to destructive vibrations. Also, the yogis say that pranayama helps to disconnect the practitioner from bodily attachment and frees the consciousness to commune with God. Pranayama can bring divine union as well as, for our purposes, increased auric power and protection. It is considered the greatest yogic method of attaining enlightenment.

Exercise: Protective Breathing

Pranayama techniques employ slow or fast breathing, breathing through alternate nostrils, or using mental images and silently intoned mantras. They are used throughout the East. For our purposes, we will employ a simple technique that will help you work with your breath and use the imagination to increase prana flow.

As I have explained, prana is our life force. Psychic people can see it as a light contained in the aura of all living things. The technique that follows has variations within Hinduism and Tibetan Buddhism; some Spiritualists and Reiki healers also use it. You will now learn how to breathe in prana (that you will imagine as light) and breath out negativity (that you will imagine as black smoke).

Step 1: It is important to ensure that you are relaxed and comfortable. If you are used to Hatha yoga (yoga postures), you may prefer to sit on the floor in the lotus posture. Alternatively, you may sit in a straight-back chair. As prana energy travels through the body along the spine, it is recommended that you sit upright to allow the energy to flow correctly. Get comfortable, but not too comfortable. Lying on the bed or flopped across the armchair will not let you get the maximum benefit.

Step 2: Now, completely relax. Let go of all tension and feel your body warmly glowing in its relaxed pose. Feel your whole body relax, from your toes to the top of your head. As you are relaxing, you will notice that your breathing slows. You feel comfortable and still within. All is peace. All is tranquillity in this beautiful moment of inner equilibrium. Spend a little time deeply relaxing.

Step 3: Focus for a while on the rising and falling of the breath. Be aware of the rhythm of the breath and how the slowing breath is increasing your inner peace. You can feel the energy within you moving. You can feel how it is removing blockages in your energy system.

Step 4: Remaining aware of the breath, you now see the air entering the lungs as a brilliant white light. It pours in and through the lungs and fills your body from your feet to your head. You are like a vessel filling with liquid light.

Step 5: Now, hold the breath for a few moments and see the light being absorbed into your body. You can feel it cleaning and replenishing you. Be aware of how vitalized you feel as the light does its work.

Step 6: Being relaxed enables you to breathe more slowly than usual. However, do not force the breath to slow down so much that you feel uncomfortable. This is not a competition. The method works best if there is no shudder to the breath. It should flow in one graceful movement from in, through hold, and then out. Under no circumstances should you gasp for breath or feel faint. Let this be a comfortable and natural process. Enjoy it.

Step 7: With the exhale, you expel all the negativity you have absorbed from other people or created for yourself. Breathing out, you relax more and more and enjoy this soothing process of self-healing. Relaxing as you breathe out quickly removes bodily tension.

Step 8: Now, breathe out slowly. As you do, imagine that the breath is now turning to black, arid smoke. These are all the toxins and negative energy that you have. You expel them from your body and give them to the infinite universe. The smoke dissolves into the great light and is itself transformed into light. You are free of negative energy.

Step 9: When you feel fully energized, finish the experiment. Sitting quietly for a while after the pranayama will allow the healing energy to be absorbed into your body and aura. At this time, I imagine that my aura is shining with a brilliant golden light. It sparkles with energy, like sunlight dancing on clear water. Permit yourself to enjoy this moment of spirituality.

The technique you have tried has many benefits. For a start, it will quickly help you to relax and become centred within. Generating a flow of prana energy releases blockages in the aura, enhances the life flow in the body, and so improves health. Cleansing the aura removes negative vibrations that may have been causing you anxiety and once sapped your energy. And, of course, the technique has strengthened your aura, making you more spiritually resilient.

Meditation is also improved when we use controlled breathing as part of our technique. If we are emotionally agitated, our breathing becomes faster, but the breath settles to a gentle rhythm when we are relaxed. This is all part of our natural "fight or flight" response. Our biological reaction to stress increases breathing, and heart rate raises blood pressure and increases adrenaline. Slowing the breath creates the opposite effect. A gentle, breathing rhythm makes the mind more peaceful. Simply taking a deep breath in a threatening situation will help you control your emotions and unthinking reactions.

Mind Fields in Business

"Prosperity is the best protector of principle."
--Mark Twain

I explained earlier how one of my work colleagues generated a negative energy that became contagious. In this instance, we were working with a very small team. However, in large organizations, the potential for discord increases dramatically. When several people work together for a common purpose, a collective "mind field" emerges. This happens within a family, between friends, within religions, in teams and other groupings and in the workplace.

Nowadays, successful businesses know that communicating with their employees is as important as communicating with the customer. When I ran my advertising/corporate communications business, I won an exciting commission from British Airways to design their internal communications campaign. My brief was to develop an internal communications campaign to build a team spirit and promote the importance of giving good customer service. We concluded that a team spirit arises if employees are treated as individuals and if their work is acknowledged as being necessary to the business as a whole. They need to feel important and appreciated. One way of achieving this recognition is with effective internal communications.

This is a straightforward premise, but once a team spirit is achieved, the ethos expands to influence every aspect of a business-- and particularly if management applies the same principles to themselves. With this comes the Holy Grail of excellent customer service, as everyone now wants the business to be a success and understands that their individual work helps to achieve this. We wrote the line "We're sold on super service" and promoted the concept with a series of "Wanted" posters to address this issue. Our idea was that teams are built when people feel their work is appreciated and that they are needed. These were targeted to every department and individual within the organization, saying things such as "Wanted: Tea ladies who take the biscuit" and "Wanted: Security men we can bank on." With these simple puns, we were able to put the message across in a friendly way without appearing to give orders. Once this was in place, the messages were reinforced through internal publications and other communications tools.

This campaign taught me the importance of building team spirit and how it can influence business success. Other qualities, such as strategy, salesmanship, incentives, leadership, and so on, are requisites for success, but all are built on the bedrock of team spirit. Without that team spirit bond, business objectives are harder to achieve. Internal marketing can act as a catalyst to encourage team building, but the best bonding takes place at the spiritual level--when people enjoy their work and feel wanted.

How many businesses understand that the phrase "team spirit" is more than a metaphor but can become a real spiritual force? Performers, trainers, teachers, trainers, preachers and anyone who works with people needs to be aware of the significance of building energy between people. A strong group aura can become a powerful force. Today we have many effective communications tools that motivate and influence people, but there are also critical hidden forces working at an unconscious level. These have been with us since primordial times.

In tribal societies, everyone must work as a unit. In pre-language societies, teamwork would have been very important, particularly in times of danger, while on a hunt or during tribal wars. A group of hunters would need to be aware of each other's position in relation to the quarry and need to anticipate each other's moves. Sometimes the chase would take place over many miles, and it would have been challenging to communicate with each other. Humans with a telepathic ability would have had the evolutionary edge. For example, hunting works best in teams, with some leading and enticing the prey and other responsible for the kill. Telepathy is a useful faculty as it enables members of the hunt to be aware of each other's thoughts and feelings over a great distance.

Telepathy makes evolutionary sense, as these qualities would assist in the tribe to survive. These shared telepathic signals helped the individuals to respond as a team. A mind-field of sustained mental energy is created and takes on a life of its own. Even after the hunt has finished, the mind field remains in place and is increased before the hunt with ceremony and ritual. The personification of these energies may account for early man's belief in gods.

Telepathic energy bonds are also beneficial to the survival of children. A child is more likely to survive if its mother understands its needs and feelings. Similarly, if those at home in the village can sense that something is wrong when a tribe is at war, they may also know whether to go to their aid or to retreat into the forest. The clairvoyant ability we call "remote viewing" would be helpful during a hunt and between members of a tribe who may sometimes need to work at a good distance from each other. Similarly, it aids survival if a person has a sense of direction or gets "gut feelings" about other members of the tribe's location.

I do not believe that our early ancestors were like telepaths from Star Trek, but they may have had an unconscious dialogue between themselves that linked them to the group's collective energy. Moreover, similar powers may be at work in our own time. A business is like a tribe. Some leave the office to hunt for opportunities or use communications tools to hunt for new business. Others tend the offices to administer the bounty. Instead of gods, we now have company logos. (Interestingly, the word "Logos" means the divine word!) There are similarities here with sales, administration roles, and the tribal roles of hunting or tending the village. The modern workplace is like a hunt--except nowadays, it is profit rather than prey that we seek. Stock-market brokers use terms such as bull, bear, and stag markets. Given that telepathy is active during the hunt, it is not surprising that it can often play a role in the modern workplace. And God only knows what the managers think when they talk about head-hunting!

I have argued that pre-language societies may have been bound by a spiritual "mind field" that enabled them to communicate individually and be aware of collective feelings. Could it be that these same spiritual energies are at work within corporate settings? My advertising and design work brought my talents to the fore in the offices of many businesses, large and small. My psychic and mediumistic powers had developed some years before I walked away from the corporate world to become a professional writer and psychic medium. During my stint and a businessman, my clairvoyant skills came in very useful. For example, I would anticipate a brief and clients would sometimes suspect that I had insider knowledge of their business plans. When we shook hands, I would become aware of my client's thoughts and get feelings about new products or services that they were planning. And, of course, it was convenient to know if they intended to pay me!

Clients would often exclaim, "How on earth did you know we were planning that!" or be pleased when I offered suggestions that confirmed ideas they were already considering. Some of my long-term clients were banks and insurance companies. Often, I would appear to have an "in-depth" understanding of the complexities of fund management and the stock market, while in reality, I knew very little indeed. The truth is, I was essentially reading their minds, to the extent of picking their brains.

I noticed that this telepathic rapport was most pronounced with clients that I liked enough to call my friends. Parapsychologists have found that telepathy works best between people who like each other. If I get along with someone in business, then we are more likely to share telepathic signals. Furthermore, the receptivity to these signals increases if we are accepted as a part of the organization's "mind field." Most of what I am describing works on an unconscious level, but awareness of these forces can improve your influence. The energy flows both ways. For instance, I found that people that had never met me before felt comfortable with me immediately. They may have liked my work and the testimonials from their colleagues, but I believe they unconsciously "knew" that I was now part of the "mind field." I had become a member of the tribe.

The collective corporate "mind field" could be described as the spirit or soul of the business. Like the ancient gods' spirit, it is an energy that is sustained and passes across the generations for as long as people continue to believe. It is as if the organization evolves its personality. I recall servicing one of my shipbuilding clients that I would describe as a "nitty-gritty, nuts-and-bolts" mind field. This mentality had worked for them since Victorian times, but now market forces pushed them to diversify from defence products. Their solution was to fill capacity by taking in orders from a manufacturer of refrigerators. The problem was that the shipbuilders' collective "mind field" was not particularly flexible, and they ended up producing fridges that would just about withstand a blast from a missile! Few within the organization realized that it was not essential to build refrigerators with reinforced plate steel; however, their conservative mind field made them blind to new ways of doing things. Fortunately, the shipbuilders soon had some big orders from the defence department and could return to building battleships. (Probably now equipped with lighting that goes out when you shut the door!) The truth is that the whole organizations can become fixed in a mind field that has outgrown its usefulness. I believe that the energy created is real and that it can sometimes be tough to change.

Job Hunting and Mind Fields

If you are looking for work or changing jobs, it is essential to let yourself become attuned to a business's "mind field." You probably already do this when you "get a feel" of what a place is like during the interview. If possible, it is helpful if the potential employer shows you around the offices or plant. In this way, you can get a better feeling of the organisation's vibrations as a whole. You may think that this is something that only psychics can do, but you probably did something similar when you bought or rented your home. You probably based your decision on how you "felt" about the property. Did it "feel, right?" When you looked around, did you "feel at home?" It is useful to allow the same gut feelings to influence you when seeking work. Ask yourself if it "feels right" to you. What sort of "personality" does the vibration of the organization bring to mind? Your responses will tell you if you are suited to the "mind field" of the organization.

There is nothing worse than finding yourself working at a job in which you feel you may never "fit in." Feeling comfortable with the organization's "mind field" is even more important than the practical things, such as wages and prospects. If you are surrounded by energy that does not suit you, you may sense that you are undergoing a continuous psychic attack. You will be spending a large part of your time in this place, and it is important that you feel in tune with the vibrations surrounding you. You do not want to feel as if you are being poisoned by an organisation's atmosphere that you will quickly come to hate.

Telepathy and Mind Fields at Work

Psychic researcher Betty Humphrey from Duke University in Durham, North Carolina, discovered that extrovert personalities exhibited telepathy better than introverts. In a business setting, the extrovert salesperson or manager is more likely to demonstrate telepathic powers and be in touch with the organisation's collective mind field. Leaders often trust their gut feeling when seeking to employ a new staff member. It is something to remember during an interview and to use to your advantage.

During the interview meeting, you may find yourself feeling exposed and unprotected, so it's useful to prepare yourself and your aura in advance. The light breathing exercise mentioned earlier may help build your energy and self-confidence. You may also use colour to enhance the strengthening effect. If you imagine breathing-in red or gold light, these can have the effect of making you feel dynamic (red) and protected (gold). It will also give you a feeling of confidence and ready for action. At the same time, your aura needs to be open so that you are receptive to signals from the would-be employers and can respond intellectually, but with one eye on the gut feelings that come from intuition.

A little soul-protection exercise before such meetings will give you a much better chance of success. When you are in the interview, project good thoughts towards your would-be employer. You may "see" them feeling happy and relaxed with their family. They will at once appear less intimidating to you, and you will be sending unconscious telepathic signals that will influence them to trust you instinctively. Once the meeting is in full swing, you will probably forget all this advice, but the commands you have given yourself will continue to work on an unconscious level. These techniques are protective and dynamic at the same time.

Psychic skills may also help in other aspects of a business. Research has shown that gamblers and risk-takers display higher than average telepathic abilities and score above chance in telepathy card-guessing tests. The archetypal risk-taking entrepreneur is likely to be unconsciously using these skills for day-to-day decisions or be aware of other organisations' mind-fields as well as his own. A "hunch" about the stock market may come from linking to the mind-field of the collective thoughts being transmitted by people at financial markets worldwide. Imaginative, creative people, particularly artists, score best in telepathy tests. Some researchers believe this is because they use predominately the right-hand side of the brain--the side also responsible   for   intuition.

The Power of Words

In addition to hidden psychic powers, we can use practical techniques to project a powerful presence. The way we dress and our body language can say a great deal about us and send unconscious signals to people we meet. Colour plays an important role, too, and we will go into this in detail later. But perhaps the most important of all are the words we use in everyday language and in business settings. Words are powerful tools that can influence others and also shield us. And how we say something can sometimes be more important than what we say.

If you own a telephone or computer, you have likely received junk calls or emails designed to encourage you to buy something you don't need or want. A great deal of thought goes into these communications to ensure you are most likely to respond. For example, while writing this chapter, a call interrupted me to sell me a new cable television service in my area. When I tried to wriggle out of the conversation, the woman presented me with a classic opening: "Aren't you interested in films?" Do you see how clever this is? Of course, I'm interested in films--as is the vast majority of the population--but the line encourages me to say "yes", and so continue the conversation. And she replies with the inevitable: "Then you will love the great films that our cable service offers." My heart sinks. How did I let her trap me? I used to use similar techniques when I ran my own business. It is incredible how few of the poor recipients of my sales messages knew what was going on. One of my favourite ways of overcoming an objection and keeping the conversation going was to say, "Don't you want your profits to rise?" A lovely hook, as they were bound to respond, and I could reply by explaining all the benefits my business could offer them.

We are constantly bombarded by advertising using this language of persuasion. Some of the most interesting I noticed being used by the BBC here in the UK when I watched the wars in the Middle East and Afghanistan unfold. The British and American forces were referred to as "our boys", and the Iraqi forces were called the "Iraqi troops." Can you see the critical point here? If we say, "fifty of our boys in the desert have been killed," it is a very emotive statement, conjuring up images of young men being murdered. However, "fifty Iraqi troops were destroyed" is a dehumanizing message. "Troops being destroyed" uses images removed from our emotions. I noticed similar language usage in the recent troubles in Afghanistan. Many of us have learned to recognize the hidden persuaders in the language that surrounds us. Words used in selling or propaganda are less likely to harm our free will if we become aware of their usage in everyday situations. Once you realize that someone is using persuasive language for a clandestine hard sell, you are in a better position to protect yourself. Listen to your inner voice, warning you to be careful. If you don't feel right about something, walk away--or refuse to commit until you are sure. "No, thanks," is always an option. Trust your inner awareness. The weapon of persuasive words can also be put to spiritual purposes. In particular, words can be used to build your own, or another's self-confidence. If you encourage another person with phrases such as, "You can do it," or "I feel you will succeed, and everything will be all right," they will be empowered to succeed and will love you for it. How often have you achieved because the people around you had faith in what you could do? It is good, also, to encourage ourselves in this way. Even negative language can be useful if we allow it to motivate us. I sometimes work better when people say I "cannot" achieve something. If someone says that I am hopeless at something, I will go out of my way to prove them wrong. I'll succeed just to spite them! On the other hand, we can perhaps learn from the Dalai Lama of Tibet. He has often publicly thanked his Chinese oppressors for giving him the spiritual opportunity to learn patience, forgiveness, and compassion. Enemies can be the best teachers.

Words can, however, invade us and cause us more harm than we care to admit. If we repeatedly say to a child, "You are completely useless. You'll never get anywhere!" is it any wonder the child fails? On the other hand, positive commands such as, "I can see you'll do fine, because you have a good head on your shoulders and loads of talent" may help your child achieve. In addition, the language places them in the future. People often find it hard to make decisions or act because they are trapped in the past or perplexed by the present. Giving them a sense of a prosperous future can empower them to move forward.

Similarly, we can use images and metaphor to help them picture their success. We can even reverse the negative language and give it a positive objective. Say, for example, someone complains that their "life is an uphill struggle." We could respond by saying, "Yes, but every day you get a little higher, and it is marvellous to rest once in a while and enjoy the view." This positive response reassures them of their progress and helps them realize that it is okay to take a break. The words we use can have a powerful hidden influence on our motivation and faith in ourselves. I remember when I was a student working on a construction site during vacations. At the time, I was having some difficulties getting the job right. Finally, I turned to my Irish ganger and said, "I'm sorry, Paddy, but I am completely hopeless at this." He looked up with a twinkle in his eye and reprimanded me in his broad Irish accent: "Don't you *ever* put yourself down, lad! There are thousands of people in the world who are queuing up to do that job for you. And they'll take great pleasure in it and do it for free, too." I still hate practical work, like building jobs or do-it-yourself projects, but my Irish guru's amusing image of a great queue of people eager to undermine me for free has certainly stayed with me. I now leave it to others to put me down, and I generally maintain self-confidence. Most importantly, his simple but powerful words protected me from myself.

Soul Protection and Relationships

"Never, never is it possible to reach someone if you become angry or bitter; only love, and gentleness can do it. Maybe not this time but maybe the next or the hundredth time."
--Cesar Chavez, Social activist (1927-1993)

British Spiritualism has seven principles, or tenants, that summarize the beliefs of mediums--one states that there is a "continual progress of the human soul." In other words, the soul is not in a static state but is continually evolving. One of the main reasons we need to protect the soul is to allow this spiritual evolution to continue. It is our birthright to have the freedom of spiritual and personal growth. Yet, during our life, we encounter many people who may inhibit this progress. We meet these people at school or at work, and sometimes they may be a partner or a member of our family.

To protect yourself from the negativity of others, it is important to observe people's behaviour and, if necessary, use persuasion to influence them. If you act from a standpoint that it is ethically right, you will feel less troubled about influencing them for the benefit of both of you. Of course, we don't want to encourage you to be a constant manipulator. Still, there are times when a situation proving uncomfortable for either of you can be influenced for the better. Using specific techniques to influence another person in this way protects you and simultaneously creates a better rapport. Enhancing our interactions with others makes and maintains good relationships.

Persuasive techniques can protect you from those who cause awkward problems. Using these techniques require you to have an objective, plan what to do or say, observe, communicate and, lastly, influence. There are many reasons to influence a person. Sometimes one person can cause havoc in a working environment, making everyone's life feel like hell. It takes teamwork to create harmony, and one person's bad energies can disrupt everything.

According to research, you are most likely to marry someone similar to yourself. This is true not only in obvious things--religion, social class, income, IQ, emotions--but some rather strange areas. Scientists have found that the length of the middle finger, the circumference of the neck and wrist, the length of the ear lobe, the lung's size, and the heart rate often "agree" in couples that get along better.

We tend to feel a kinship with people that mirror ourselves. Because of this, it is possible to influence a person by subtly reflecting their gestures. This must be done very carefully, as someone can take offence by mimicry. Yet, a person in an excited state of mind may appreciate you more if you reflect this urgency of attitude. Similarly, someone who is depressed would be easier to reach by responding in a soft and gentle voice. Reflecting their behaviour can reinforce the bond between you, as long as it is done very subtly. When people are really "in tune" with one another, they often do the same things at the same time and even breath to the same rhythm. You can use this to increase rapport and make a person feel at ease by reflecting their body language. For example, on a romantic date, if they are leaning at the bar, you lean too. When they lift their glass, lift yours at the same time or soon afterwards. When they sit down, you sit down. If they fold their hands, fold your hands as well, although with perhaps a slight delay, so it is not apparent what you are doing. Try to be subtle. Do not mimic parrot-fashion.

For example, if they cross their legs, you cross your ankles.

At the same time, you may also reflect the other person's language, speaking with similar metaphors or images. People think differently and are orientated to their senses in different ways; for example, you may think in pictures (seeing), words (hearing) or feeling (sensing). You are probably a mixture of all three, but one is likely to dominate. Suppose you respond to someone by saying, "*I see* where you're coming from" or "I get the *picture*" or "Let's get things in *perspective.*" You're more likely someone who thinks visually.

If you tend to say "I *hear* what you're *saying*" or "That *rings* a bell", or "You're *speaking* my *language,*" you most likely think in sound. However, if you respond with "I can *handle* this", "I get your *drift*", or "I *feel* the same," you likely think with your feelings.

By listening carefully when a person speaks, you will soon notice that they tend to use terms relating to a particular sense. Once you have figured that out, you can respond in kind. So, to flatter a person who is a visual thinker, you will say, "You've really *brightened* up my day", or "We *look* good together" or "You make me *shine.*"

Similarly, in talking to a verbal thinker, you will use words like "We're on the same *wavelength*" or "You're really *chirpy*" or "We seem to *click.*" With a sensory person, you will find yourself using touch words, "You're really *warm*" or "I like your *pushiness*", or "I'm glad we made *contact.*"

Certain qualities identify the orientation of a person's thinking habits. A visual thinker tends to speak quickly, miss details, and often speak in a higher-pitched voice. They will use words that refer to seeing, imagination, and colour. They tend to look upwards while thinking, keep an erect posture, and possibly have jerky movements. Verbal thinkers have a smooth language that flows like music. They use words that refer to hearing, speaking, and listening. Their eyes move from side to side when they think. They keep their head square, have flowing gestures, and keep an upright posture. The sensory thinker speaks quietly and slowly with long pauses. They use words that refer to touching, such as feel, touch, hold, heavy. They look down while thinking, like to make physical contact, and slouch slightly.

Putting matching techniques into practice may help you to develop a better rapport with people. They can be used to make bonds that will help you solve the day-to-day problems of human relationships. These simple methods can be used to calm people down, bring them out of depression, encourage or motivate, and help you get your messages across. Once a good rapport is established, it is easy for people to work together without conflict. Awareness brings understanding and, with it, spontaneous protection against the negativity of loaded relationships.

Of course, similar techniques can be used when a rapport would not be helpful, such as when someone is wasting your time or talking too much. Similarly, if a discussion has reached an impasse or you are being harassed and want to bring the interaction to a conclusion. In such instances, you simply reverse the technique and do the opposite to what the person is doing.

Being aware of how people think, and responding accordingly, can actuate them in positive ways. You can exert quite an influence if the person believes that you think the same way they do. They find themselves responding to you but do not quite know why. I also think that it is possible to enlist our intuitive abilities to help a person achieve a more positive attitude. In this case, we do not need to say or do anything. Positive thoughts about the person given from the heart will help them. They will connect to the vibrations we give to the "oneness" or interconnectedness of all beings. When we are willing to share of ourselves and give from the heart, we set in motion a natural process of inner transformation that functions according to each person's intuition.

Strong Relationships

Today we are gaining a greater appreciation for the axiom of "oneness," that all beings may be spiritually interconnected. During the first part of our life on earth, we are merged with our mother while in the womb. It takes some time after birth before we experience ourselves as something separate. For example, learning to tell lies and keep secrets are two important ways for a child to discover that its mind and mothers can be distinct. Some psychologists believe that many people, without knowing why, seek to return to this state of worry-free existence. Perhaps, they hope to escape the responsibility of individuality and return to the blissful oneness that they knew before birth. Sometimes we rediscover this innocent state when we fall in love. We become childlike, holding hands, calling each other silly pet names, and playing as without care when we are with our sweetheart. This is a natural part of the bonding process.

I have observed that many people who come to me for clairvoyant consultations are hoping to find romantic love as a way of escaping from troubled lives. They want someone to come into their lives and make all their decisions for them, giving up all personal responsibility. At clairvoyant consultations, they often look to me to wave a magic wand and make all their troubles evaporate, perfectly willing to exchange personal responsibility for a destiny that will supply everything they need and want. They wish to sit back and wait for it to happen. If the first clairvoyant does not give them the answers they need, they move to the next and the next until they hear what they want to hear.

A good clairvoyant will advise clients to take responsibility for their lives, for this is the only true way to happiness. A clairvoyant may help them see more clearly the lay of the land, but the journey into the future is up to them. Insights about the future may provide guidance, alerting the client to potential hazards and developing opportunities, but never be a substitute for free will. Happiness comes from feeling secure and in control of our lives. Similarly, a happy relationship is achieved when both individuals allow themselves to act like one yet still retain their personal responsibility. They stand like two columns in a temple. If the columns stand too close or far apart, the building will collapse. But if each column is strong, the structure will endure with the right amount of space between them.

If people sacrifice self-reliance within a relationship, it is not surprising that they expose themselves to many problems and disappointments. Relationships are an opportunity for growth. It is a mistake to use them to escape responsibility. They offer the opportunity for our hidden potential to flower, protected within the garden of family security. A good relationship is a spiritual opportunity for two people to help one another up the ladder of soul evolution. A loving relationship protects and fortifies both partners and is the bedrock of the family. In turn, family values founded on love nourish children's hearts, who become the hope for a better world. These fortuitous circumstances increase the family's positive energy, thereby protecting the soul and enabling spiritual progress.

Vibrations Between Couples

There are many reasons that people are attracted to each other. During courtship, many bodily and emotional signals come into play that help to bind the couple together. The result is, of course, a sexual union that, in the best case, results in marriage or lasting partnership. But there are also spiritual forces at work that intensify this coupling. It has been found, in laboratory experiments, that telepathy works best if there is a rapport between everyone working on the investigations. For example, the number of correct guesses of Zener cards increases if the "sender" and "receiver" like each other and increases dramatically if they love each other. When we are in love, we share thoughts more readily. A loving couple becomes like one unit, yet they still maintain their own identity and free will.

Many people feel most vulnerable to psychic attack at night. From a psychological standpoint, this is the time when we are most tired and therefore less able to deal with problems. Is it not often the case that our troubles persist and press upon us most relentlessly when we are tired? Isn't that when we tend to worry the most? This is the time when you are most likely to get into a quarrel with your partner or lose your patience with an irritable child. At the end of a long hard day, you are less likely to be able to manage your emotions and feelings.

The primary purpose of sleep and dreams may be to quell the emotions, to keep them from overheating. Dreams allow the emotions to express themselves in the language of allegory, metaphor and symbol. They help us to "cool down." Troubles that may have fired us with emotion in the evening seem not half so bad after a night's sleep. Tiredness is often the cause of many unintended words and actions.

During the evening, I try not to think about things that worry me. They can all wait until the next day when I will be far more able to find positive solutions to the issues that require my attention. When we sleep, our dreams are in the background of our awareness, helping to solve our problems. Even if we do not recall a dream when we wake up, the solution to a problem often becomes clear in the morning. So, if you have problems, do not try to solve them late at night, or have intense head-to-heads with friends or loved ones. Give yourself time to allow the tiredness and stress to settle. If you have a decision to make or a problem to solve, sleep on it. It is remarkable how often the solution to the problem appears self-evident in the morning.

As night approaches, we may feel emotionally susceptible if we become involved in a quarrel. We are also more likely to say things that we do not mean. This is not the time to "sort things out once and for all." Domestic violence and suicide are all the more likely at night. Nighttime arguments are also more likely to penetrate aura fields, and this can affect you profoundly. When negative energy is freely exchanged, both are the worse for it.

Sleeping with your partner without resolving an argument can seriously disrupt inner harmony. Negative energy may unwittingly be exchanged even while sleeping. Try to resolve disputes in the cold light of the morning, and at least have a truce in place before you go to sleep. If this is not possible, as you prepare to sleep, draw your aura in towards the body, reducing your susceptibility to the other person's vibrations. This can best be achieved by imagining the auric light pulling back to the body. As it does this, you may see the aura forming a strong protective shell around you. I usually imagine that I am sleeping in a full suit of armour.

On the one hand, this helps to strengthen and protect my auric field. It is also such an amusing image that it takes the edge off my anger. Even soul mates have a tiff from time to time, so when it happens, use this technique to safeguard your aura energy and allow you some "personal space" while your emotions calm down.

Self-Awareness

"One moon shows in every pool; in every pool, the one moon."
--Zen Forest Saying

I have spoken about the importance of being aware of what motivates other people and how to protect yourself from their negative vibrations, but are you aware of what motivates you? It is easy to blame all of our troubles on others, but what if our thoughts are the greatest enemy to the progress of our soul.

If we feel pressured by the vibrations of another person, it can set up a cycle of negativity in ourselves. We can turn from the victim of a dispute into the perpetrator of the problem. It is important to protect ourselves from others' negativity, but it is also important not to fight such bad vibrations with our own brand of bad vibrations. Once there is a cycle of hate in place between couples, friends, or colleagues, someone must work to break that cycle. In most instances, this responsibility is likely to fall to you.

Ignorance and a lack of self-awareness are responsible for a great deal of the suffering that besets us. Fortunately, this is something that can be overcome entirely. A good start is to consider learning a meditation technique so that you learn to separate yourself from your thoughts. In daily life, the anxieties of our heart or the confusion of our mind directs our actions and inner disposition. At times, we may behave like saints; at other times, we are like monkeys.

Most spiritual disciplines' objective is to train us to develop better virtues and human values and replace ignorance with direct knowledge of the divine. Through these disciplines, we gain knowledge and learn to live with compassion. In this way, we become a better person, and our heart shines with the light of love. The souls of people who have reached this high level of spiritual development are protected by the light of their own spiritual energy. For the rest of us, it takes a little work.

It would take thousands of books to show how to control the mind and allow the heart to shine. There are so many different people in the world that thousands of religions and mystical teachings have inevitably arisen to cater to this individually. What may be right for one person is not necessarily the best path for another. Nonetheless, I believe that the key to spiritual development is self-knowledge. By this, I mean knowledge of our strengths and weaknesses and the knowledge of the soul. We discover that we must turn our attention within. In most instances, this is achieved through meditation.

In meditation, we discover how to step back from the turmoil of our everyday thoughts and just watch the inner drama unfold. Eventually, the restlessness of our thoughts begins to settle, and the inner world becomes calm and peaceful. The internal state has been likened to a glass of muddy water that is continually agitated by desires. However, when we step back and just watch the mind, the thoughts, like the muddy water, becomes still. When this happens, the mud settles to the bottom, leaving the water crystal clear. Inner clarity is achieved when we let the mind and the emotions settle.

During these times of inner quietude, we can also connect to our soul's prompting and be in touch with our inner voice. As a Spiritualist medium, I believe we meet in meditation our spirit guides and mentors from the next world. They connect to us via our intuition and innermost thoughts and feeling. For example, while monitoring the stream of thought in meditation, you may become aware of other people's thoughts and the thoughts of people in the spirit world. As the mind becomes very quiet, it is much easier to distinguish these thoughts from your own. In meditation, the mind can be likened to a still pool wherein even the smallest stone cast will show ripples. Similarly, the stilled mind brought on by deep meditation allows the subtle influences from other realms to be more easily observed.

Angels of Protection

"Angel of God, my guardian dear, To whom God's love commits me here; Ever this day (or night), be at my side, To light, to guard, to rule and guide. Amen."
--Traditional Nursery Rhyme

If you believe in the reality of the afterlife, you may accept the possibility of drawing upon its beings to protect you in your day-to-day life. In particular, many believe that angels can come to our aid, but you must ask them. They can be relied on in times of crisis or despair and react to our distress. Angelologists claim that there are many hierarchies of angels and that each angel has a designated purpose. For each crisis of ordinary life, there is an angel, so to speak, "on call." For example, if you needed help so your garden would flourish, you would ask the angel called Risnuch for his blessing.

Today, many people believe that angels watch over us in a spirit of love and come to our aid when we are in danger. There are also workshops available to help you attune yourself to these spiritual mentors. To make the connection, a person is advised first to become "grounded." To do this, angelologists advise you to centre the attention on the body and be aware of the present moment. The objective is to help you gather your mental energies and remain focused. You then enter the "releasing" state, in which you let go of worries and negativity and find release in the sense of unconditional love. There is then an "aligning" period to attune yourself to the vibrations of angels. In this open state of relaxed awareness, you are asked to listen within, for the voice of your protective angel speaking to you through your intuition. This final stage is called "conversing."

The above exercise is often done as a group meditation, perhaps with simple rituals such as lighting incense and candles, ringing bells, playing music, saying prayers or reciting affirmations. The angelologist may face the four directions and chant various incantations or Psalms to invoke the multiple angels by name. Also considered necessary is the time of day. Although frogs and swords were used in such rituals in medieval days, today's angelologist focuses mainly on invoking thoughts of well-being and harmony to open communications with the next world.

I am not one for ritual myself, but I can see how such techniques can help some people get into the right frame of mind and centre their meditations. We see this in both religion and magic. In my work as a medium, I often feel spirit helpers draw close while I am demonstrating or in meditation. Many of these spirits are familiar to me, such as family members that have passed over. Similarly, I may feel my personal spirit guides' closeness, who have helped me over the years to perfect my gifts. There are also times when I feel beings of light around me. Although they are unfamiliar to me, they radiate great love, peace, and protection. I don't know their names, but there are times I am sure that I am in the presence of angels.

Your Special Angels

Angelologists believe that a guardian angel and a clerical angel are assigned to each person when that soul decides to incarnate. This belief holds in many different religions, cultures, and societies. The angels are charged with our protection throughout our earthly lives and may intervene if we call upon them. The guardian angel is the one who assists a spirit/soul in planning what is to be learned and experienced while in bodily form. They set the "lessons" of life. The clerical angel is responsible for writing down those lesson plans and documenting what the spirit/soul experiences--entering the good and the evil deeds done into the book of your life. The "Life Book" is the spiritual record held within the cosmic memory of the universe.

These two angels never leave and never part the incarnated spirit/soul--from the time they are "born" to the time they "die." All angels are not specifically concerned with the affairs of humans, having other responsibilities. For example, Cherubim, Thrones, and Principalities are charged solely with watching and protecting Earth and aspects of the Universe. Many angelologists believe, though views differ that the guardian spirits or angels are the only ones who have the duty of protecting and watching us. These are, in turn, assisted by the legions of Archangels. Some mediums I have worked with will call upon angels when clearing malevolent spirits that may be causing trouble. Also, they ask their own personal "spirit guides and helpers" to draw close for protection. For many, the Archangel Michael is the primary one to call on for protection and strength. Understandably, he is the patron of police officers. Some call upon Michael and other higher angels for general protection under challenging circumstances. The ten most well-known angels are: Michael, protector of the North and the guardian of peace; Gabriel, protector of the South, who brings strength, hope, and revelation; Uriel, protector of the East, said to bring new beginnings and social reform; Raphael, the healing angel, who is the protector of the West. Raphael is also the guardian of our physical bodies. Also, Metatron, the angel of fire and celestial scribe; Moroni, the angel of the Latter-day Saints; Melchizedek, believed to be the father of the seven Elohim Angels; Ariel, the "Lion of God" who rules the waters; Israfel, the angel of resurrection and song; and finally Raziel, who proclaims the secrets of men to all mankind.

Contrary to popular belief, we do not speak to angels with our minds or hearts but through our soul's attunement. It is when we touch this innermost, eternal part of ourselves that we connect with these celestial beings. For me, meditation provides the opportunity to make this connection. Others may prefer some form of ritual or ceremony to help them get into a proper mindset. For example, an affirmation or statement may be used to call upon a guardian angel. A person with an illness may say, "I am ill. I call upon my guardians to make me well because I have important work to do, and others depend upon me." Angels are said to respond to altruistic intent and those who trust in their power to help.

You may call upon the angels as part of your daily routine. You may, for example, ask that a day be free of difficulties or without stress. I have one friend who calls upon the angels whenever he needs a parking space. Remarkably, it appears to work! The routines you use to reach your angel can be as simple or as complex as you like. Some may say elaborate incantations or do rituals of manifestation using candles inscribed with symbols to represent the angel called. It is up to the taste of the person and their beliefs and practices.

Angelologists also consider many angels to have specific protective roles. The listing of angels given here come from many traditions but are in no way complete. All, however, can be called upon for protection. I have highlighted here angels with specific protective roles to help primarily with everyday situations:

Adnachiel is supposed to protect those born under the star sign of Sagittarius.

Ambriel is considered an angel of general protection and particularly suitable for those born under Gemini. This angel also inspires clear communication and the ability to speak the truth.

Angels of Crescent Moon and the Throne Class. These are supposed to be invoked to bring animal protection. Angels linked to this protection ring are Behemiel, Hariel, Thegri, Mtniel, Jehiel, Manakel.

Aralim is claimed to bring protection to the home and loved ones.

Barchiel is the angel that rules the sun signs of Scorpio and Pisces.

Cambiel This angel is the ruler of the zodiacal sign Aquarius. Invocations to Cambiel will also bring increased intelligence and provide unusual solutions to problems.

Esme is a protecting angel from Wales UK.

Giel is the angel that will protect those born under the sun sign of Gemini.

Haqadesh is invoked to prevent a psychic attack and protects you from people drain your energy

Hayyel Protects wild animals. Included in this ring are the angels Thuriel, Mtniel and Jehiel.

Hngel is the angel of the summer equinox and protects against the evil eye.

Ielahiah protects magistrates and brings justice in legal matters.

Ioelet protects during an exorcism.

Isma'il also protects during exorcism rites. Governs a group of angels that can take the guise of cows.

Jerazol is an angel of power that is invoked during conjuring rites.

Kmiel protects against the evil eye and is used in some Jewish amulets.

Lazai is an angel that is invoked in the exorcism of fire.

Leliel is one of the protectors during the night.

Mehiel protects university professors, orators and authors.

Mumiah will suspend physical laws and create miracles.

Muriel protects those born under the sign of Cancer.

Natiel has the power to ward off evil and is sometimes found in lucky charms.

Nehinah can act as a protector for mediums.

Olinda is the protector of property in some German traditions.

Ophiel protects during meditation.

Paniel is found in charms to ward of evil. It also protects against the North Wind.

Paschar protects during unconsciousness.

Phakiel is another protector of the sign of Cancer.

Qafsiel is invoked by writing his name in bird's blood and was used in Hebrew magic to drive away enemies.

Ramona is a Teutonic angel that protects the wise.

Sabreael protects against demons that bring disease.

Schaltiel protects the sign of Virgo.

Sosol is invoked in some magic rites and is said to protect those born under the sign of Scorpio.

Teiaiel gives insight into the future and protects maritime expeditions and commercial ventures.

Tzaphqiel is a general protector against all evil.

Ubaviel is one of the guardians of Capricorn.

Urpaniel is an angel from the East whose name is used in magic charms.

Vehuiah will fulfil prayers for help.

Xexor is a benevolent spirit invoked in conjuring rites.

Yahel will reveal secrets and protects against clandestine plots.

Zuriel protects those born under the sign of Libra.

6 PROTECTING THE AURA

"All things flow, nothing abides"
-- **Heraclitus**

I have explained that the aura is part of an energy field surrounding living things and links us all together, something like a Spiritual Internet. We've talked about how this energy can connect us to people with positive or negative energy, or to groups who have created a "mind field" of collective energy. I've also told you that the energy that fuels the aura can take shape, as independent thought-forms imbued with a life of their own. And I have spoken about how thought is not imprisoned within our brains but can influence the world around us and play a part in the energy we attract. Now, I will explain how the aura can be used to protect spiritual work, such as mediumship, and how to use it in everyday life situations.

According to yogic theory, humans exist in both a physical and a subtle or astral form. The subtle body encases the soul and will carry it into the next life. While living in the physical body, the subtle body radiates its energy in the "light" that psychics see surrounding living things. This light--which is, in effect, a manifestation of our life force--we call the aura. The aura has also been described as the "human energy field."

The subtle body/aura has it's own "anatomy," one that is distinct from but related to the physical body. The subtle system consists of three nadis and seven chakras. There is a network of 72,000 nadis, which are the channels along which prana (life energy) flows. Many of these are given specific names and correspond to the meridians in acupuncture. The most important of these is the central channel, or Sushumna, which runs down the midline of the body and along which are located seven energy centres called the chakras.

The chakras are where prana energy is focused. In Sanskrit, the word "chakra" means wheel; and it is seen by clairvoyants as wheels of light. The chakras are positioned up the spine from the base. Each of the seven chakras has several spiritual qualities. All the chakras play a role in our spiritual well-being, but in some people, specific chakras are more dominant than in others.

The lowest chakra, called the Muladhara chakra, is located at the base of the spine. It is linked with the legs and the dense parts of the body, such as the bones. It is associated with physical survival, and a person centred on this chakra may have anxieties about money, shelter, and material things in general. The next chakra, the Swadhishtana chakra, is sometimes called the spleen or solar centre. It is associated with the reproductive organs, bladder, and kidneys. A person centred on this chakra may be emotional and have high sexual energy. Next comes the Malipura chakra, which corresponds to the solar plexus. It is associated with the back and the digestive system. A person centred on this chakra can be creative but also has a lot of ambition. The Anahata chakra, the fourth chakra, is located at the centre of the chest and associated with the heart and lungs. A person centred on this chakra will have qualities of hope, love, and devotion.

The next three chakras correspond to spirituality and the search for enlightenment. In my work as a medium, I have noticed that these three sometimes work as a unit. They are responsible for the various aspects of clairvoyance and ESP. The first of these is the Vihuddha chakra (fifth chakra) located at the throat. It is associated with the lungs, neck, vocal cords, and speech. It corresponds with the qualities of clairaudience, communication, discrimination, and expression. Next is the Ajna chakra, located in the middle of the forehead, associated with the mind, face, and pituitary gland. This is the centre of contemplation and spiritual insight. Finally, the highest chakra, the seventh, is called the Sahasrara chakra. It is located at the crown of the head and is symbolized by the 1,000-petal lotus. It represents cosmic consciousness and the infinite.

Good health is achieved when the nadis allow the free flow of prana energy between the chakras. However, yoga teaches that the balance and flow of prana can be interrupted by many things, including your emotions, state of mind, past actions (karma), and your current preoccupations. Your sleeping pattern, the way you breathe, the exercise you do, and your diet also affect the prana's flow through the nadis and into the chakras and aura. All of these things can be improved by yogic exercises, proper breathing, and meditation.

Protective Colour

"Yellow is capable of charming God."
--**Vincent Van Gogh**

Each chakra has a colour associated with it, corresponding to its traits. The chakra colours appearing in the aura indicate a person's state of mind. If I see red in someone's aura, I'm alerted that he or she may be feeling aggressive. The red colouring, however, can also indicate a sexually active state of mind. Therefore, my response to the person must be based not only on what I see in the aura but what my gut feelings are telling me about the individual.

While not everyone sees or senses the aura, we are all influenced by it. We respond to the auric vibrations of others, and they respond to our subtle vibrations. All life exchanges auric energy. I also believe that we intuitively know which colours our aura needs, and we sometimes use colour to compensate for this lack. For example, we may impulsively buy brightly coloured clothing because, at the time, the colour is lacking in our aura. Dressing to compensate for a colour--or alternately to enhance a colour--will influence our thinking and encourage the energy vibrations associated with that colour to manifest in the aura. It is likely that, once an auric imbalance is restored, we may never want to wear the clothes again.

Colour can help to protect the aura. For example, if you feel vulnerable or anxious, it is best to dress in a powerful colour to compensate for what is likely missing in your auric energy field. An intense colour, such as red, not only makes a statement, "Danger, here I come," but helps build up a positive-power energy vibration. In voodoo magic, Feng Shui, and many tribal cultures, red is a sacred and protective colour. In the aura, it is the colour of dynamic energy associated with blood and the life force. Your unconscious mind knows which colours are lacking in your aura. The colour may not usually be your favourite, but it is the one that is needed to restore your balance.

Colours can have many meanings, varying between cultures and age groups. For example, children tend to like bright, happy colours. Westerners wear black as proper funeral attire, while in Japan, white has this association. While colour symbolism varies greatly, auric colours are universal and show a great deal about a person's psychology. Colour not only influences our feelings and mind but stimulates what is spiritual in us--and the aura that reflects that spirit. We will now take up the meanings of the auric colours and how to use them for spiritual protection.

THE COLOUR RED
Associated with the Base Chakra

This is a powerful colour; hence red is a good colour to use when you are feeling down. It helps to raise your energy levels. The auras of athletes often display red--the colour of physical fitness--, so if you feel a lack of red in your aura, exercise may help you build it up. On the other hand, if this colour expresses how you are feeling right now, perhaps you need to calm down. We've all heard of "seeing red" when angry. In this instance, one could change the vibration by actively visualizing the opposite colour, green, which is calming. Red is a symbol of strong emotions rather than intellectual ideas. It can reveal excitement, energy, strength, danger, passion, and aggression

THE COLOUR ORANGE
Associated with the Spleen Chakra

Orange controls the aura around the spleen, which psychics consider the cleansing and energy distribution centre. A lack of orange in the aura means that you may need an excellent emotional tonic. You need stimulation. Force yourself to go out and enjoy yourself socially until you feel your vitality return. Orange is a perfect colour to use when you need to find balance in your life. As a symbol, orange can represent energy, warmth, enthusiasm, and flamboyance.

THE COLOUR YELLOW
Associated with the Solar Plexus Chakra

Yellow auric light is associated with the area around the solar plexus. It controls the digestive processes of the body and the creative faculties of the mind. It is linked to the solar chakra that can store our energy, yet it also gives us ambition and motivation. If you feel the need for this colour, you may have been working too hard at work or concentrating too hard on a decision. Yellow is also an optimistic colour, like a ray of sunshine. Use this colour to stop worrying and bring new optimism into your life.

THE COLOUR GREEN
Associated with the Heart Chakra

A need for nature's colour means that you are seeking peace and harmony. This is one of the primary healing colours particularly if the tone of green is emerald. Green is associated with the area around the heart. Being drawn to this colour expresses a need for getting in touch with your innermost feelings. Use green to find rest and inner harmony. Green brings the restorative power of nature. Very pale greens are sometimes associated with illness, envy, and naivety, while superstition considers this colour unlucky to wear. However, a rich tone of green or the green seen in a rainbow are life-enhancing colours.

THE COLOUR BLUE
Associated with the Throat Chakra

Healers often have the colour blue in their aura. A lack of this colour in the aura denotes a need to slow down--concentrate on letting your body and mind find their natural harmony. If you've been over-excited lately, try to relax with some music, or just put your feet up. Blue decor is ideal for giving or receiving healing energy. Sky blue, sometimes called Madonna blue, is associated by some people with the feminine archetype of the divine mother. Blue can also symbolize peace, calm, stability, security, loyalty, sky, water, cold, technology, and depression. Blue is believed to transform and diffuse negative energies gently. It is an excellent colour to work with for those whose approach to life is receptive and gentle.

THE COLOUR INDIGO
Associated with the Forehead Chakra

Indigo auric light is connected with psychic abilities. You may enjoy taking an interest in the paranormal or extra-sensory perception. Your attention wants to turn inwards. Indigo is a good colour to use during meditation. With indigo associated with the unconscious, you might understand yourself better if you wrote down your dreams and tried to learn what is on your sleeping mind. The intense auric colour of indigo denotes a time for contemplation and renewed self-awareness. This is the time to listen and receive guidance from the inner self.

THE COLOUR VIOLET
Associated with the Crown Chakra

Violet is a spiritual colour. If you feel a draw that indicates this colour is lacking in your aura, now may be the time to start a spiritual discipline. Forget your material worries for a while, focus on the higher things in life, and work to deepen your inner stability and harmony. I've noticed that vegetarians' aura often has a violet hue so that dietary considerations may be important. Associated with the highest energy of the godhead, violet is favoured by many psychics as the most protective colour. Like purple, this colour can symbolize royalty, nobility, ceremony, mysterious, wisdom, enlightenment, and mourning in its darker form.

Other important colours not directly associated with specific chakras:

THE COLOUR BROWN

Although it is usually the brighter hues that are seen by psychics in the aura, brown may feel important to you for psychological reasons. Brown is a strong colour--the colour of the earth. Brown symbolizes the earth, hearth, home, the outdoors, comfort, endurance, simplicity, and comfort. You would benefit most by concentrating on practical solutions to life's problems. Brown is useful for grounding or centring.

THE COLOUR BLACK

Black is the absence of light. It can act as a protective shield around the aura if you feel overly sensitive and will seal you from negative vibrations. On the other hand, you may be feeling a lack of colour in your aura. Instead of needing more black, your aura may need brightening up a bit. Imagine that you radiate a rainbow of lights all around your body and see if you soon feel your spirits rise. Colour can help lift depression. In China, black represents the passive female energy that nurtures and supports all things. Slimming and stylish, it is one of my favourite colours to wear.

THE COLOUR WHITE

Purity and vitality are implied by the colour white. It is the colour of spiritual energy and in China symbolizes the masculine creative force called Yang. If you feel your aura needs this colour, you may be seeking divine inspiration. Re-establish your contact with your core beliefs; "Know thyself," as the saying goes. Perhaps, too, you have been taking life a bit too seriously. Humor and laughter are God's best medicine. White also reflects all colours, so has the effect of returning whatever is sent its way.

THE COLOUR SILVER

Silver's mirroring effect can be used to protect against negative energy being projected by others. Like white, the reflecting quality of silver allows others to recognize and understand the impact their thoughts and actions have on others. I associate the silver colour with humour, having noticed that people with a silvery aura often have a witty disposition and can laugh at themselves.

THE COLOUR GOLD

Gold is associated with success and is the colour of the heavens. It is the sacred metal of religion and, as alchemy's spiritual goal, represents the perfect soul. Gold will consume any energy that is not in harmony with it. Mystics believe that it is beneficial to those who are extroverted and have a positive outlook on life. The use of the colour gold is most appropriate in situations where one is surrounded by disturbing energy.

Colour Breathing and Visualization

"Most people think that ageing is irreversible and we know that there are mechanisms even in the human machinery that allow for the reversal of ageing, through correction of diet, through anti-oxidants, through the removal of toxins from the body, through exercise, through yoga and breathing techniques, and meditation."

--Deepak Chopra

Ancient Eastern traditions tell us that the aura is composed of life energy; some call this energy *prana*, and some call it *chi*. This energy can be released and increased by particular practices that cleanse and allow the free flow of this energy through the physical and subtle bodies. By expanding the life-force energy within the aura, we enhance our vitality, health and awareness.

A simple method to stimulate the aura is to draw energy into the body through the breath, as we did earlier, except that now you use coloured light to draw upon the particular vibration of energy you need at the time. You can try this now. Or it can be done at any time, when you're in a hurry, feeling tired, or just need extra energy. The way to do this is to imagine that the air you slowly breathe in is not air but brilliant light. You are drawing upon the omnipresent life force that is everywhere, in everything and is inexhaustible. You can choose white light or one of the colours just mentioned. The colour you choose to breathe in will fill you with the qualities we described above.

Hold the breath for a few seconds and feel the light flood your whole being. Notice how the colour reaches every part of you, bringing about a sense of well-being, balance and composure. Now slowly breathe out. Imagine the air as acrid smoke, removing the toxins from your body and your mind.

Repeat the cleansing breath a few times. This exercise can quickly revitalize your mind and body, and your aura will fill with the colour qualities you need. If you are travelling to a sales conference, you may wish to breathe in a communicative colour such as yellow. If you are feeling tired, you may want to breathe in white light to refresh your energy. If you need physical energy, you may try inhaling red light. Peace of mind comes with indigo light, and for healing, try blue or green. Silver is good protection to reflect negative energy, and gold is believed to act as a protective shield for the aura.

There are many techniques available to help you strengthen and protect the aura by visualizing colour. Many people like to work with the green heart chakra that lies in the centre of the chest. This is the seat of compassion and universal love. Imagine that a light is shining in this centre. At first, it is small, like the flickering light of a candle, but as you give it your attention, the light grows in intensity. The candle now becomes like a light bulb. You are illuminated from within with a brilliant white light shining from the centre of your chest. Feel the joy as this centre awakens. Feel your expanding unconditional love for all living things. Let go into the bliss of love.

The light bulb now becomes brighter and brighter until it is like the sun. It shines with a magnificent radiance. Its life-giving warmth enfolds you. There is nowhere within you that darkness can exist. Every facet of your being is infused with the life force. The power of love removes every resistance. The radiant energy that flows through you finds no obstructions. The aura is complete. Each part sings in perfect harmony. You are whole. Your life is one, united in the light of love.

This simple meditation will clear all negativity that is being projected at you, for it calls upon the power of God and embraces the universal unity of all life. Whenever I begin a period of meditation, I start by sending positive thoughts to those I love. I then follow this by sending positive thoughts to those with whom I have problems, and finally to all living things. By doing this, I free myself from both good and bad attachments, and my meditation can proceed in a way unencumbered by my life ties.

Some people prefer to use a less expansive technique. For example, a good aura-building exercise is to imagine you are sitting in an egg of light. The narrower end of the egg extends below you, just into the ground so that you are linked to the energy of Mother Earth. You now imagine that you are surrounded in your egg by a lovely protective colour. Gold, silver, violet or blue are favoured colours by many, though we found that coral pink generated a feeling of security and protection in our group. You now imagine that your eggshell is solid so that no negative energy can get through.

The inside of the egg is now filled with coral light, and you feel as if you are again in the protected waters of the womb. Nothing can harm you, and you are at perfect peace. For a while, you remain in this state and bask in the restorative energy, knowing that for a while nothing can harm you. All the negativity you have within yourself is channelled below, into the earth. In this way, your energy and inner composure are restored, and you are better prepared to deal with life when you return to everyday awareness.

These techniques can be used alone but are particularly effective when you work with a group of people, with one talking the rest through the group visualization. In this way, you not only empower yourself, but these energies are enhanced by the shared power of the people working with you.

Using colour and cosmetics

People have some funny ideas about colour. For example, the Masi tribe believe that black gums are attractive; the Lala of Nigeria think red skin blemishes are lovely. Lots of tribes believe the most beautiful bodies are those covered in colourful tattoos. Many of the body markings and face paintings of tribal societies were used as ritual magic and fertility rites. Often they were used to protect the wearer from evil spirits.

The colours of cosmetics we use form a relationship with the aura.

Today people wear makeup to make them look attractive to others and give themselves a feeling of self-confidence. When "Kolor Cosmetics," one of Britain's most prominent cosmetics outlets, heard about my interest in colour and the aura, they commissioned me to advise them in these areas. Colour and the aura was then used as part of their marketing campaign. It proved to be an exciting and fun project that demonstrated in a very practical way how the theory of colour and the aura can be used in daily life.

As explained, the colours in an aura can reveal a lot about that person's health and personality--including mood traits. For example, someone with a lot of yellow in the aura tends to be cheerful, optimistic, and often very creative. The colours we wear, as clothes and makeup, can influence both our conscious and subconscious moods and subtly alter the colour of our aura. The deliberate use of colour in your dress and makeup can give you a feeling of self-confidence in situations where you may typically feel exposed.

The key is using colour to positively change the way we feel and the image we project to others. The aura is powerful about the head, so it makes sense to think about the colours we choose to wear on our faces. The colour of a woman's facial cosmetics will influence her mood and subsequently change her aura colours. It could be argued that colours worn on the body have a stronger influence than those in a person's environment or clothing.

Certain colours will have a specific effect and fine-tune the way you are feeling. For example, if you are in need of a pick-me-up, wearing a bright-coloured item of clothing--red, for instance--could make all the difference, as will applying a brighter lip colour, as red is a sexual colour. When red is seen in the aura, that person means business, while the colour pink is associated with pregnancy.

The colours we wear can also influence the colours we project to the other person. If red is already dominant in a person's aura, it could mean there is a feeling of anger, so I would recommend avoiding red altogether and using a more balanced shade, like green or brown. Brown is a very safe, stable colour. It's often found around people who don't want to be rushed. People with silver auras are usually fun, with a good sense of humour. It's an excellent colour to add when in a party mood, topping it off with silvery and glittery eye makeup.

As cosmetics are all about looking good and influencing the opposite sex, we naturally looked at how colour can influence relationships. For example, orange and yellow are happy colours and have a cleansing effect on the aura. They can help long-term partners to laugh with each other or attract a cheerful man to a single woman. However, orange is also a colour that is considered outrageous. Green will show that you are balanced and looking for a stable relationship; blue will also, to some extent, although blue can also mean that you have lots of energy. Royal blue is aggressive yet chic. Violet is a sign of spirituality; great for anyone who has found or is actively searching for their soul mate. Dress in red, and it's a good bet you're looking for a companion for the evening. Mix in a bit of laughter, too, with sparkly colours like silver and gold, associated with energy and fun.

Auric Light

"Be near me when my light is low, When the blood creeps, and the nerves prick and tingle; and the heart is sick, And all the wheels of Being slow..."
--Lord Alfred Tennyson

For a medium to sense subtle vibrations, the aura must be "opened." In effect, this means letting down our natural spiritual protection and allowing ourselves to become aware of the influences that come to us through the sixth sense. A person's aura is naturally protected during ordinary awareness, and it is not easy for vibrations to penetrate. The aura that surrounds the body is shaped like an egg standing on its narrower end. An analogy would be that, during everyday awareness, the egg has its shell on. When we "tune in" to use our spiritual powers, the shell is removed, and the aura expands. Naturally, this leaves the person vulnerable to potential harmful vibrations, so there are a number of safeguards that the psychic or medium uses as protection while working.

After all that was said in previous chapters about mind fields, negative energy, voodoo, and so on, you would think it is a perilous thing to open the aura and subject yourself to unknown spirit forces. However, if mediumship is practised in the right setting, with the right people, and most importantly, for the right motive, then it is perfectly safe. I would, however, suggest that, in the early stages of mediumistic development, practitioners sit with others rather than be alone. The collective power of a group acts as natural protection so that mediumship can be practised safely. Also, I would not recommend the use of coquina boards or lancets. These may bring quick and exciting results, but the results can be disastrous. Only very skilled mediums use these devices, and even then, most mediums consider them clumsy and misguiding.

When you sit with spiritual people who have good intentions, it is possible for mediumistic awareness to flower. Not everyone may have the potential; instead, psychic and healing gifts may unfold, and these are of great benefit in the service of the soul. So long as the intention is right, the energy the group generates will act as natural protection from potentially harmful entities. I remind my own students that "darkness cannot penetrate light" and that if they work with light and love in their hearts, they will never come to harm while practising the clairvoyant arts. Besides, I encourage a cheerful and lighthearted atmosphere, as this not only aids mediumship but is also a powerful light-building technique. If a spirit of love and laughter resides within my group, I know that we will have good results.

To open the aura, we use a special technique that raises the energy up the spine to the crown of the head. The method asks you to visualize that there is a sea of light below you. You then visualize that the light from this sparkling sea is rising up through the chakras one by one until it extends out of the top of the head. As the light rises through each of the chakras, they open like flowers of light. Once this happens, a light falls from above and pours down through the body and aura, cleansing your energy field. The aura now expands, filling with the liquid light that rains down. Eventually, you feel vitalized and well, as the aura opens to its full potential. Throughout an evening's practise, we know how the aura is being continually replenished from the cosmic source that surrounds and permeates all things.

Some people come to my circles to enjoy the healing and inspiring effect of this auric light. The power of the energy in the room can lift a person's worries and depressions and can heal the body, mind, and soul. Many come just to enjoy basking in the light or to allow the energy to flow through them to help those who are developing their mediumship. These energy workers are acting in a spirit of service and kinship that makes for fertile ground for the seeds of mediumship to grow. Once the work is finished, it is necessary to close the aura down. How this is done will be explained later in this section.

A fully expanded and opened aura enables the people working together to share their auric energy and use it to communicate with the spirit world or practice other spiritual gifts such as healing, clairvoyance, or precognition. This energy increases when people work together, as we collectively draw from the Cosmic Source mentioned earlier. I tell my students that, while working, they should not rely on their energy but draw from the cosmic energy and the group's energy. I point out that the auric power we have to work with conforms to the maxim "The whole is greater than the sum of its parts." This is particularly important when spiritual healing; healers must not use their own auric energy or are in danger of becoming ill themselves. They should instead allow energy to flow *through* them rather than *from* them, in this way connecting to the life-force energy that is everywhere and in all things. A physicist may liken this to connecting with the zero-point energy described by quantum physics that proposes that unlimited energy is available from any point in space. (Others would bite my head off at the very thought that mysticism and science could have any parity!)

When we share energy in the way I have described, many beautiful things are possible. Collective energy can be used to heal people, particularly those who feel that they have been subjected to psychic attack. A person coming to a collective healing session would not necessarily need to be involved in the meditation process of opening the aura to benefit from the experience. The group simply directs their healing powers to that person. We may, for example, ask person needing healing to sit in the middle of the group so that we can more easily direct healing energy to them from our now energized auras.

I spend a lot of time teaching my students to move auric energy. Being able to move this energy consciously allows it to flow spontaneously whenever we work spiritually. This is essential to the skills of healing and mediumship. When we meditate, we sit in a circle. One method employed is to visualize auric energy moving first clockwise and then in an anti-clockwise direction. It is incredible sometimes to sense the feeling of power that builds in the room when we do this simple exercise.

Similarly, I show my students how to move their energy by holding their hands apart and bringing them together in the praying hands' position. As the hands gradually come together, I ask them first to imagine a pushing sensation between the hands and then, on the next try, to imagine a pulling sensation between the hands. This gives a strange sensation, like the attraction or repelling of two identical or opposite magnetic poles. Eventually, I teach my students to see the aura's light and consciously move the light seen between the hands. Once several have learned to awaken their auric sight, we are able to try many fascinating and startling experiments that can eventually be seen by all of the participants. Generating auric lights and balls of auric light in this way is an early form of physical mediumship. It has resulted in the formation of a small amount of ectoplasm during my trance work. (Ectoplasm is a visible mist-like substance that flows from a medium. Some of the great mediums were able to build this spiritual material into the full-size human form of the spirit communicators. Alas, my powers do not extend to this at the time of writing.)

When we have finished working in the circle, it is important to close the aura down to protect one's sensitivity and prevent exposure to everyday life's many negative vibrations. It is like putting the shell back on the egg. Again, detailed instructions are in the sources mentioned earlier. At this time, the participants imagine the chakras becoming quiet and still. The crown centre remains open while the light and energy quiet around the remaining chakras. The energy is seen to drop down through the chakras one at a time, returning finally to the sea of light below. When the chakras are quiet, we feel and see a brilliant light from above washing through our aura, rinsing away any remaining negative vibrations we may have. Then we see the light filling us like a vessel, but this time the chakras remain closed. Finally, we close the chakra at the crown and return to normal awareness.

I also recommend another simple safeguard to ensure that the chakras are closed: imagine that you are wearing a dark, hooded cloak. You wrap it all around you and, as you do this, you see the aura drawing in close to the body. This helps the aura to shut down as you return to normal awareness. In addition, this useful protective technique can be used at any time. For example, if you feel exposed or worry that your aura may be vulnerable, use this visualization to enclose and safeguard yourself quickly. Once you are used to practising this visualization in a circle setting, it is easy to do in an emergency, having become a protective habit.

Becoming a Medium

"If you don't ask, you don't get."
--Gandhi

If you embark on the path of mediumistic development, there will be many changes to your body, mind, and spirit. Some Spiritualists say that mediums often gain weight if they work with trance or physical mediumship as a large body is required to produce ectoplasm. Many believe that mediums must watch their sugar intake as mediumship depletes the body of sugar and can cause diabetes if the sugar is not replaced immediately after working. Also, it is said that during the first stages of mediumistic development, a person's sexual urges can swing between the extremes of wanton desire to complete loss of interest.

Much of this may be hearsay, but I believe that the body needs to be protected while working with mediumship. My solution is to practice basic Hatha Yoga. These physical exercises were designed thousands of years ago, not just as a health system but to prepare the body for the monumental inner changes that happen when a person takes yoga's inner journey to enlightenment. I do not have space here to go into detail, but there are plenty of books available about yoga. I would encourage all mediums who are serious with their work to practice yoga to protect their bodies when working with mediumship.

Many inner changes also happen to people when they work with these higher functions of the soul. There can be many troubling questions to be resolved, and a person is often made to confront many difficult inner problems. In recent years, mediumship has become fashionable again, causing many people to claim to be mediums. It is hard sometimes to know who is a real medium and who is not. However, a real medium will have been through terrible tests that come to them as part of their development. Although these are inner changes, circumstances will have arrived that have forced them to make those internal changes. For some, it may have been an awful childhood; others, dilemmas faced later in life. The catalyst for spiritual transformation may be the death of a loved one, illness, bankruptcy, or a whole host of unthinkable problems. These troubles, however, do not serve to break the person but rather teach the medium about suffering and how to find the inner modesty required before gifts can be bestowed on them. All the true mediums I know have suffered badly at some time in their lives, tested to their limit.

As mediumship flowers, there are also many changes to the soul. These transformations begin before we are born and are made in consultation with our guiding mentors in the afterlife. I mentioned earlier that we are "forced" along the path, but this is not the case. The troubles encountered by mediums happen because the soul knows what it needs to be done even when the neophyte medium is entirely unaware of his or her destiny. The lower mind and body may rebel sometimes, but the higher purpose is eventually achieved despite weaknesses. The medium, nonetheless, has a choice in these things and can at any stage return to ordinary life if they so wish. This combination of inspiration and suffering is the spirit's driving force, and I believe it to be the hallmark of the true spiritual teacher.

The perilous path of mediumistic development usually moulds a person into someone who is both resilient and sensitive. In particular, the aura can now open and expand more than the ordinary person, so enabling the medium to commune with the spirit. At first, it can be tough for new mediums to protect themselves from our everyday world's negative vibrations. With such auric training as mentioned above, they soon learn how to switch their powers on and off at will.

I often say to my students that it is not the dead you need to worry about but the vibrations of living that can cause you the most trouble. If you can learn to protect yourself from this world's negativity, dealing with any negative influences from the spirit world is a cinch.

Three things protect a medium:

1) **MOTIVATION.** The right intent is fundamental to safe mediumship. People who fool around with coquina boards or try to develop mediumship for egotistical reasons will have problems. Necromancy and the summoning or casting out of demons is also a dangerous path. Genuine mediumship is done with a spirit of service and with the intent of helping the bereaved and inspiring us to a greater understanding of the nature of reality. The sincerity of purpose, coupled with the proper study, is the foundation upon which to build these gifts.

2) **ENERGY.** The aura is the vehicle for the soul and also its protection. Understanding how to open and close the aura enables mediums to work only when they want to. When the aura is closed, no spiritual forces can intrude. Mediums are then able to live ordinary lives. Similarly, developing positive thinking and good human values purifies the aura. In particular, the energy of cheerfulness and humour can generate a great protective force.

3) **SPIRIT GUIDANCE.** The unfoldment of mediumship happens with help from an individual's spirit guides and helpers, usually within a development circle's safety. These spirit people also

protect the medium's work in the years to come.

I will explain how the spirit guides work with us in a moment, but first, let us consider the areas in which a medium needs protection:

EVIL SPIRITS.

Some people use the fear of evil spirits to make a fast buck. Superstitious people may think that evil spirits are to blame for illness, bad luck, and a host of misfortunes. There are many "magicians" who claim they can and will remove these influences-- for a price. Moreover, some seemingly religious people--who put money before morals--use the fear of demons to raise funds for their affluent preaching lifestyle.

Although evil spirits may exist, they are not as common as these con men would have us believe. Sometimes spirits are misguided but are not evil as such. They are people--just like us--except they now have no body. Even mischievous spirits are good at heart. I have met many people who claim that an evil spirit is harming them, but closer inspection reveals it to be the result of an overactive imagination. In a few cases I have encountered, a real spirit can be involved, but all these usually require is some guidance and to be made aware that they are "dead." Most of the claims about evil spirits are nonsense. One of my mediumistic colleagues aptly commented, "If it were possible for mediums to be attacked by such beings, then there would be no mediums working!"

LOST SOULS:

This is another area where there is a great deal of misunderstanding. Souls do not get "lost" per se. Sometimes a person in the spirit may be confused, not realizing that they have died. They are upset because they think that the person they are trying to reach is ignoring them. Similarly, it may take the spirit person time to awaken to what has happened, so they remain for a short while in a somnambulistic state of awareness. Eventually, they will awaken to the knowledge of the higher life and the loved ones waiting to greet them. Indeed, a medium--or anyone else--has nothing to fear from such "lost souls."

THOUGHT FORMS:

I have already explained these in detail. Thought forms are energy fields that have established independent existence but no separate consciousness. To dissipate these, we need to remove fear from our mind and not feed the energy field with our attention. These fields are very rare phenomena and need not worry mediums. An energy field cannot harm you. Similarly, Mind Fields are energies that surround an individual, a group of people, or an organization, but these cannot cause serious harm to a medium.

HAUNTINGS AND POLTERGEISTS:

These are often thought-forms. A poltergeist may be the expression of repressed psychological energy. Hauntings are often a build-up of negative energy, perhaps caused by someone who has been thrust into the spirit without realising what has happened. A medium can often help in this regard by speaking to them and encouraging them to go with the spirit people waiting to help them. Again, there is nothing here that would harm the medium.

POSSESSION:

At no time -even while in a trance- can a medium be taken over by a spirit against his or her will. Most cases of possession are, in fact, a form of psychological obsession. These cases consist mainly of people of weak minds who have either convinced themselves that they are possessed or suffer from schizophrenia. In a few rare cases, the influence may be caused by a mischievous spirit who takes advantage of any mental imbalance to draw close. Such a spirit, however, cannot possess a person's body--there is no room.

Spirit Guides and Helpers

"A teacher affects eternity; he can never tell where his influence stops."
~ Henry Brooks Adams

Spirit guides and helpers are beings from the afterlife worlds who have chosen to help others on their path to enlightenment. In the case of mediums, these beings aid in communication with the next world and protecting the mediums in their charge. Most of these spirit guides and helpers have had previous lives on the earth plane, and they may have spent a great deal of time in the spirit world preparing to work with the medium. In my case, I believe I have known my guides from previous lives and the time I have spent in the afterlife between earthly incarnations. It could be argued that these guides could be aspects of myself that have become splintered from my own personality. I do not believe this to be the case, and I have been presented with evidence to suggest otherwise (some of which can be found in my book *What to Do When You Are Dead*).

From the communications I have received, it appears that spirit guides are not enlightened beings; they admit to many imperfections. They speak wisdom yet retain modesty and humour. Guides may remain with you for a lifetime or stay for just a short period. The "gatekeeper" is believed to be the individual's main soul guide; that is, there when we come into life and there when it is time to die. The "gatekeeper" is usually somewhere in the background as one of the primary guides in a person's life.

Unfortunately, some people get a bit carried away with this "guide" thing. At this moment in time, it is very fashionable to have a spirit guide, and often people who are not really mediums make all sorts of pronouncements about who is your spirit guide. Some people claim to have a totem animal guide. I do not have this myself, but I suppose it may be of use to people who need to call upon an animal spirit--for hunting and other such purposes. Unfortunately, this type of thing can get entirely out of hand. I watched one "medium" working, who claimed to give messages from animal guides, give outrageous statements from talking hamsters! Similarly, I know mediums who give messages from just about every guide under the sun or make a big deal about having a higher guide than the next person. Again, caution is required.

The guides are manifestations of the beings of light that help us from the next life. They take a form that we can recognize, but this form is not as important as the messages of wisdom that they bring. Nonetheless, certain traditions were more inclined to become helpers in the next life when their time came to die. For example, many Spiritualists believe that the exterminated American Indian tribes continue their spiritual traditions in the next world. In this world, they lived very close to the spirit world, so it was easy, and normal and natural for them to become the intermediaries from the next world.

I know who my guides are, but that is not important. I know they are there when I work, and they interject when I make mistakes, or my ego gets too inflated. I have no idea whether my guides are higher or lower than the next person's. Frankly, it does not matter. They are all beings of light and only come in the guise of a physical form so that I can recognize them. Does it matter if a guide is an American Indian, a Zulu or a High Priest of Atlantis? As far as I am concerned, they can appear as Mickey Mouse if they want--just so long as the mediumship is done properly!

When I first developed as a medium, I felt it a little embarrassing to talk about spirit guides. I would have entirely understood anyone who thought I was "a bit cracked." Indeed, because of my circumstances, it was necessary to keep my work as a Spiritualist secret. It would have been frowned upon in my work at the time, and it is only very recently that people have been more open to such things. Even today, it is still difficult to talk about mediumship openly on the BBC, and there are many ITC rulings and restraints still in place, as I write today in the year 2002.

The practice of mediumship has only been legal in the UK since 1956. For example, the physical medium Helen Duncan was jailed after a court case held in the Criminal Courts at the Old Bailey in 1944, when she was tried under the ancient Witchcraft Act of 1735!

I have several spirit guides that work with me as I do my mediumship. I have never had anything negative or worrying come through as I work, so I presume they must protect me from potentially harmful influences. If protection is needed at all, I can rely on them to keep unwanted influences away from my aura, but their primary role is in organizing the communications coming through. Imagine what it must be like on the spirit side when a medium is about to demonstrate to an audience? The possible spirit contacts that could be made are many thousands when you consider all the family members and friends known by the audience. Yet, the spirit communications come through in an orderly fashion, with only the right spirit links given to specific people in the audience.

Without the spirit guides' organisation and protection, the communications would become very chaotic and probably wholly unintelligible. Before I start a demonstration, I always hear my guide's voice instruct me, "Now, remember to let us do the work. Don't interfere, and just give what we tell you." So long as I follow their instructions and repeat what I am told, the mediumship is clear and precise. I simply go with the flow. If, however, I think to myself, "Oh, that can't be right, they must mean..." then the accuracy of my mediumship falters. We mediums learn to put our complete trust in our guides and helpers. Only when we are able to do this can our mediumship become accurate enough to give empirical proof of life after death.

Trust in the protective power of the guides is particularly important when working in a trance. This is when I am very vulnerable, yet never has there been a problem with unwanted spirits entering me. Again, this is another area where there is a great deal of misunderstanding. Although my guide and people known to my sitters can speak directly through me, at no time am I completely "taken over." In the first stages of my trance, I am aware of myself speaking. I can hear my voice, but it appears to fade completely into the background. I am in a state of complete disinterest when the guide and others are speaking through me. It is like a monotonous voice in the distance. However, I am aware that I am in a trance and can pull myself back to everyday awareness instantly.

Naturally, mediumship requires proper training from a qualified Spiritualist, a recognized medium, or another recognized organization (such as Sprites or the Swedenborgh movement). When mediumship is conducted in the right conditions, the right energy, with the right motives, and with the spirit guides' assistance, then it is perfectly safe, and you are well protected.

7 SPIRITUAL CONSIDERATIONS

"God gave us two ends. One to sit on and one to think with. Success depends on which one you use; head you win--tails, you lose."
--**Anonymous**

Could it be that whatever we see in others is only a reflection of our own self? Very often, we blame others for our faults and vice versa. Often our impressions about another person are a reflection of our feelings towards them. I mentioned this in the section where I spoke about the shadow, and I believe it is one of the main reasons people extend negativity in everyday life. The truth is that our impressions of people--and perhaps our impressions about everything we know of the world--is just a reaction and resound of our inner state. Maybe we should question ourselves when we find fault in another. Is this fault perhaps an echo of something we dislike about ourselves or a reaction to our own weakness? Similarly, when people criticize us unduly, maybe we can spot hidden motivations and inner weakness in that person.

Do we have the right to find fault in another? Our assessment is limited to our single experience of him or her. There are many aspects of our adversary's personality that we do not know, so we cannot truly judge them. Every person is a mixture of high and low consciousness. There are times when I stand in front of large crowds and melt their hearts with my talks about human values, spirituality, and mediumship. There are many instances where I have acted from the right motivation and high moral principle. Yet there are also times when I can be petty and childish and behave like a jackass! Aren't we all a bit like this? We are all a mixture of high and low.

The East's wisdom describes this lower self as the "monkey mind," and only the fully enlightened are free of it. The monkey mind is motivated by selfish desire and can interfere unexpectedly in all our lives. The analogy may come from the way they catch monkeys in India. A small pot is left outside near an area where monkeys live. It has a small opening and is filled with some sweets or solid fruit. When a monkey spots the sweets, he puts his hand inside the pot and grabs a big handful. But, alas, his greed is such that he cannot get his full hand out through the opening. Even when the person who set the trap approaches, the monkey will not loosen his grip. He is bound to his desire!

In the same way, desire holds us to this world. It is the source of most of the negativity that I have described in this book. The outer world is the pot, and the situations in life are like the narrow opening. Like the monkey, we try to grab what is good from the world, but we sacrifice our freedom in so doing. We blame the world for our imprisonment, but the irony is that we enslave ourselves by our refusal to let go of desire. If we can shed this desire, then we will live in the world freely.

It is the "monkey mind" that is the enemy within ourselves and also in others. When qualities such as envy, anger, greed, revenge, lust, and so on arise in a person, the monkey mind wants to grab the sweets for itself. There is a conflict in people between the spiritual essence and the lower mind. By taming the monkey mind and overcoming our greed and desires, we find a way to free ourselves from the material world and set foot on the path to the eternal.

At the beginning of this chapter, I said that what we see in others is a reflection of ourselves. I understand that when we let ourselves fall victim to our own monkey mind, then we bring out the monkey mind in other people, too. Have you noticed this? And it is not only our observable behaviour that does this, but our thoughts also appear to influence others' behaviour. I have spoken about how telepathy affects other people, but could this also be part of the cosmic interconnectedness that I spoke about? Call me paranoid, but I believe that whatever goes on inside our heads changes the reactions of people around us and the world itself. Our thoughts and desires pluck the threads of the cosmic mycelium, and these vibrations change the world around us and future trends.

The truth is that we generate our misfortunes and "lessons." These arise due to our actions and thoughts in this life, but we also may carry forward positive and negative potentials from previous incarnations. In the East, they call this law of cause and effect by the name "Karma." It can be summarized in the words of Jesus when he said, "As ye sow, so shall ye reap." Karma could be thought of as one's destiny or fate, which has to be worked in your life. This law may account for why we sometimes encounter situations similar to previous problems we had. "Oh, no! Here we go again!" we may say, as once again we seem to face a crisis or situation that is almost a clone of what went before. We think that destiny has it in for us and that we are like the monkey, caught by a wandering beggar, dancing at the end of a rope. But just like the monkey-with-the-jar karma is of our own making, we can free ourselves from our potential destiny if we simply manage to let go of what binds us. Perennial wisdom teaches us that we can free ourselves from the bind of karma instantly if, instead of being the slave of the senses, we make the mind the servant of God.

Spiritual Protection

The progress of our soul is in our own hands. We can protect the soul and guide its course if we master the monkey mind and regulate our conduct. In this way, the goal of enlightenment is won, for we move away from desire and focus on the supreme reality. I believe that this is the way to protect the soul and that it is the meaning and purpose of life. Until we realize the divine in our nature, the world will press on us and sometimes nearly suffocate us. But once the goal of liberation is achieved--the monkey lets go of the sweets--the world will fall away, and freedom is achieved.

Working to develop our spirituality not only protects our life now but our future as well. Indeed, as someone who knows the afterlife to be a reality, I would argue that this life should be used to make us into better people. What we do now determines our spiritual progress in the future, including the length of time we may spend in the afterlife and the quality of our future incarnations on earth.

We can protect ourselves from the world's negative influences, but, more importantly, we must protect ourselves from ourselves.

Our ignorance and selfish desire are the monkeys that must be trained. This training requires spiritual work, and the nature of this work will vary from person to person. For one person, yoga and meditation may be the path; for another, it may be prayer or service to others. I try my best to be observant of myself and correct myself when necessary in my ordinary life. The method I favour was told to me in India. The guru explains that one should think of this maxim every time we look at our wristwatch: "WATCH = Watch your Words, watch your Actions, watch your Thoughts, watch your Character, watch your Heart." Self-observation is undoubtedly a splendid and easy way to control that monkey mind.

Now, everything I have written above sounds fine, but many people do not give a hoot about spirituality in the real world. They spend a good part of their time catering to the needs of the monkey mind. There are many instances in my life where I have acted spiritually, with the good of others at heart, and been betrayed. Harm can come at unexpected times, and from people you think you can trust. Even our loved ones fall into error and can be moody, irritable, jealous, unreasonable, and sometimes downright nasty. The monkey mind plays tricks all the time; we see its selfish ways arise in many everyday situations, and it is responsible for most of the negativity that I have mentioned here.

Sometimes we take ourselves too seriously, and the ego causes harm. We forget that we are playing a role in reality, like an actor on the stage and that our true self is not what we put on display to the world but lies somewhere behind the mask. That true self is the soul, forever shining behind the complex game of life. Sometimes the world may appear to be filled with darkness and negative energies, but this is only because we are clouded to the truth. In reality, the soul shines all the time, like the sun in the sky. It is our true nature, and it is full of light and love. If we look, we can see it everywhere: in the face of a child, in a loved one or friend, in the eyes of an animal, and even behind the glare of our enemy. Life is a game played in a dream. When we awake, we will see that nothing can harm the soul, for its light can dissipate the darkness, and its wisdom can tame the monkey within us. When the light of the soul is allowed to shine, we are protected from real harm.

ABOUT THE AUTHOR

Craig Hamilton-Parker is a British author, television personality and professional psychic medium. He is best known for his TV shows *Our Psychic Family*, *The Spirit of Diana* and *Nightmares Decoded*. On television, he usually works with his wife Jane Hamilton-Parker, who is also a psychic medium. Their work was showcased in a three-part documentary on the BBC called *Mediums Talking to the Dead*. Craig has also made films about India's ancient oracles in the movie *Mystic Journey to India*, which is now available on Amazon Prime.

Craig and Jane now have TV shows in the USA and spend a lot of time demonstrating mediumship worldwide. They have a hugely popular weekly show on YouTube.

Born in Southampton, UK, Craig was convinced at an early age that he was mediumistic. He became well known as a platform medium within Spiritualism. In 1994 left his job as an advertising executive to become the resident psychic on Channel 4 television's *The Big Breakfast* making predictions for upcoming news stories. He wrote a regular psychic advice column for *The Scottish Daily Record* and regular features for *The Daily Mail*, *Sunday Mirror* and *The People*.

AUTHOR'S WEBSITE: **psychics.co.uk**

PUBLISHED BOOKS

Hamilton-Parker, Craig & Jane (1995) *The Psychic Workbook* Random House ISBN 0-09-179086-7 (Languages: English, Chinese)

Hamilton-Parker, Craig (1996) *Your Psychic Powers* Hodder & Stoughton ISBN 0-340-67417-2 (Languages: English)

Hamilton-Parker, Craig (1999) *Timeless Wisdom of the Tibetans* Hodder & Stoughton ISBN 0-340-70483-7 (Languages: English)

Hamilton-Parker, Craig (1999) *The Psychic Casebook* Blandford/Sterling ISBN 0-7137-2755-1 (Languages: English, Turkish)

Hamilton-Parker, Craig (1999) *The Hidden Meaning of Dreams* Sterling imprint Barnes & Noble ISBN 0-8069-7773-6 (Languages: English, Spanish, Portuguese, Russian, Israeli, Greek Icelandic.)

Hamilton-Parker, Craig (2000) *Remembering Your Dreams* Sterling imprint Barnes & Noble ISBN 0-8069-4343-2

Hamilton-Parker, Craig (2000) *Unlock Your Secret Dreams* Sterling imprint Barnes & Noble ISBN 1-4027-0316-3

Hamilton-Parker, Craig (2002) *Fantasy Dreaming Sterling* imprint Barnes & Noble ISBN 0-8069-5478-7

Hamilton-Parker, Craig (2003) *Protecting the Soul* Sterling imprint Barnes & Noble ISBN 0-8069-8719-7

Hamilton-Parker, Craig (2004) *Psychic Dreaming* Sterling imprint Barnes & Noble ISBN 1-4027-0474-7

Hamilton-Parker, Craig (2005) *Opening to the Other Side* Sterling imprint Barnes & Noble ISBN 1-4027-1346-0

Hamilton-Parker, Craig (2010) *What To Do When You Are Dead* Sterling imprint Barnes & Noble ISBN 978-1-4027-7660-1 (Languages: English, Dutch, Portuguese)

In this book, I reveal the secrets of the Indian Naadi Oracle that tells me that new spiritual knowledge will be revealed to me by the gods – which I initially interpreted as my mediumship – and from studying the Naadis, learning astrology, and knowledge given to me by living rishis. This book is a startling insight into the nature of destiny and the future of ourselves and the world.

AVAILABLE FROM AMAZON OR
THE AUTHOR'S WEBSITE: PSYCHICS.CO.UK

The book will show you how to recognise your latent abilities and develop your psychic and mediumistic skills. It shows you how to set up your own psychic circle and offers sure-fire techniques that will enable you to develop a highly accurate mediumship.

AVAILABLE FROM AMAZON OR
THE AUTHOR'S WEBSITE: PSYCHICS.CO.UK

Printed in Poland
by Amazon Fulfillment
Poland Sp. z o.o., Wrocław

76114798R00091